Sabbaticaleer

Your Best Job Ever – Build a Sabbatical That Lasts

Will Thomason

Kintsugi Publishing

ISBN: 979-8-9960279-1-0

Published by Kintsugi Publishing

Also available as an ebook

For my family —
my beautiful wife Elizabeth
and our amazing children, William and Grace.

And for my parents,
Woo and Bill Thomason,
gone too soon.

Contents

Preface	VII
Prelude - The Legend of Kintsugi - An Allegory	XI
Introduction	XIV
1. The SPiCE of Your Life	1
2. Knowledge vs Narrative	20
3. Purpose: Aim High from Solid Ground	34
4. Image vs Identity	48
5. Self-Reflection and Metrics Planning	57
6. Ancient System, Modern Wisdom	74
7. Best Practices: Reset Your Mindset	88
8. Systems that Stick	99
9. Time to Brainstorm your Sabbatical!	110
10. A Sabbatical that Lasts	124
11. Filter your Fulcrums	142
12. Envisioning Your Second Act with Legacy in Mind	150
13. Your Sabbatical Strategy Brief	160

14. The World Needs More Heroes 169

Epilogue 186

Appendix I - Glossary 193

Appendix II – The Sovereignty Triangle & Journal Prompts 199

Appendix III - Selected Sabbatical Reading 213

Acknowledgements 224

About the author 226

Preface

"The best job you'll ever have."
– Richard W.

That's what Richard, my last CEO, said to me the day I told him I was thinking about taking a sabbatical. It marked the beginning of my own sabbatical journey, which started the following year.

And he was right.

A sabbatical is the best job you'll ever have, because the job you're taking on is you. And you're the boss.

But make no mistake: while a sabbatical can be the most satisfying job, it's not a glorified vacation. It's about investing dedicated time and energy to dive into your own deep waters and purposefully realign for your second act in life. As the boss, you set the rules and boundaries. And no matter how long you plan for, sabbatical time goes fast. Best you make the most of it!

That's where this book comes in. It's not an autobiography of my sabbatical. It's an introduction to *yours*. It is a pay-it-forward knowledge transfer of the best practices and strategies I wish I'd had – practical tools to help you design and execute your own successful sabbatical. Solid ground, no matter what circumstances bring you here, as you consider giving yourself the gift of a lifetime: "Your best job ever."

Welcome to *Sabbaticaleer*: Your Best Job Ever – Build a Sabbatical That Lasts

The word *Sabbaticaleer* is inspired by my childhood love of *The Three Musketeers*. Those brave, honorable, and skilled soldiers faced the world together with strong camaraderie and a ready sword and musket. In the same spirit, a Sabbaticaleer is someone who successfully embarks on a sabbatical and continues to benefit from it long after the official time off ends.

In these pages I will introduce you to *SPiCE* — *Sabbaticaleer's* simple but powerful acronym for the five core pillars of your personal ecosystem: **Spiritual**, **Physical**, **Intellectual**, **Currencies** (what you treasure), and **Emotional** well-being. This framework served as the pumping heart and holistic backbone of my own sabbatical. Combined with nearly three decades of strategy and brand-building experience, *Sabbaticaleer* is here to help you build your own customized, trackable sabbatical plan that sets you up for a purposeful and lasting second act.

This book is your practical companion and trusted mentor rolled into one. It gives you the tools to build a sabbatical plan that fits your life, plus the real-life lessons I learned on my own 321-day sabbatical journey and beyond. I hope that, just as the mentors I respected helped me prepare, *Sabbaticaleer* helps you approach your sabbatical with confidence and come out the other side with a second act that feels purposeful, balanced, and unmistakably yours.

Wherever you are right now — just considering the idea, actively prepping, or already on your sabbatical — this book meets you exactly where you stand.

Sabbaticaleer has been in the making for more than a decade. Because I woke up one day and my own SPiCE reserves were on life support after the unexpected happened. My wife got stuck in a multi-year cycle of incapacitating illness exacerbated by misdiagnosis and ill-advised treatments. We had two young children. My work suffered. Then, my parents unexpectedly died in a freak carbon monoxide accident. My well-curated world was falling apart all around me. I was worn out and distracted. The center wasn't holding. I wrote in my journal at the time: "I begin my sabbatical at the crossroads of a blessed life and tragedy. I arrive exhausted, hoping to recharge and shift gears into a new phase of my life."

Until then, I had enjoyed a successful advertising career. It had been fun and challenging, and I was very good at it for a long time. As an agency partner, I was fortunate to lead a stable of national brands and work on our new business team. We were a privately held agency in charge of our destiny, competing on a national stage. It was energizing.

I'm grateful I had a CEO like Richard when my sh!t hit the fan. I could count on him to talk straight with me about both professional and personal matters. He had always positioned himself as a strong Servant Leader – someone who leads by serving others first, putting the growth, well-being, and success of his team ahead of his own, with humility, empathy, and genuine care. And he lived up to it. He was there for me with sincerity, objectivity, and support.

When I decided to pursue a sabbatical, I was determined to bring my strategy, branding, and research expertise to bear on my own restoration and rebranding experience. The earliest outline for this book was the cornerstone of my personal experience, informed by the advice and expertise of trusted friends and colleagues, as well as my sabbatical research.

Something brought you to a place where a sabbatical is on the table. Life has its own agenda. I had never imagined myself doing anything else until I walked into the office one day and realized that I saw myself both doing something else and needing to do something else. With that, my sabbatical had a momentum all on its own.

So ask yourself: why a sabbatical? What's going on now?

Personally, I knew I would be no good to anyone if I didn't take the time to heal and realign myself. It's like the flight attendant's instruction: put your own oxygen mask on first, so you're equipped to help those around you. Sabbatical beckoned, and I took the call seriously.

You'll have your own reasons. Chances are, a sabbatical may be for you, but it isn't realistic now. You may need to wait until the end of the fiscal year, a child graduating, or any number of things that require you to get your ducks in a row so you can pursue your sabbatical with reduced stress. Or maybe the time is now, and you're ready to get started. That is awesome!

That's it for the Preface. Whether you're serious about a sabbatical right now or still navigating calendars, budgets, or other circumstances but see a potential sabbatical in your future, this is a book for you. Your second act calls!

With gratitude, I'm here to pay it forward. I envy you as you embark on your sabbatical adventure! Good luck!

Prelude - The Legend of Kintsugi - An Allegory

Long ago, in a kingdom far away, an Emperor prepared for the coronation of his only son, Kintsugi, as Crown Prince. His reign had brought peace and prosperity to all—rich and poor, peasant and highborn—who traveled from near and far to celebrate.

The Emperor was wise and holy. He taught his son the truths passed down from his own father: reject passivity, accept responsibility, lead courageously, and expect God's reward. To honor the occasion, he commissioned a magnificent crown of pure gold, intricate and radiant.

Word of its beauty spread, drawing gifts from every corner of the realm. One gift stood above the rest: a chalice crafted by the Emperor's oldest friend and most trusted advisor. It shimmered with a heavenly translucence in torchlight and sunlight alike. The Emperor placed it on display beside the crown, ready for the ceremonial toast to his son.

Then, disaster struck.

The day before the coronation, the court discovered the prized chalice shattered on the floor. Prince Kintsugi stood by his father, seeing the shock and sadness in his eyes. They gathered the pieces gently and set them beside the crown. The banquet that night was subdued. Everyone retired fitfully, dreading the morning.

Then came worse news.

Word raced through the palace and beyond: the broken chalice and the crown were gone. How could thieves—or fate—have taken both? The ceremony would have to be delayed; a new crown forged. Despair settled like fog.

Moreover, Prince Kintsugi had locked himself in his quarters with only fiery sounds of fury reverberating behind the closed doors. All entry was barred, and all pleas were ignored. A dark cloud hovered over the court. Was this a horrible omen?

The people urged the Emperor to console his son, but he only offered a wistful smile. For two long days, no coronation—just the muffled roar from those locked chambers.

On the third morning, another enormous commotion filled the Great Hall. People pressed forward to witness the impossible—someone had returned the chalice and crown. But now, if possible, the chalice was even more beautiful than before, restored with rich veins of the purest gold filling the cracks that had once defined its brokenness, and by its side rested a new crown, a simple but elegant band of woven gold.

That evening, everyone gathered in the Great Hall and witnessed a scorched but resilient Kintsugi enter and kneel before his Emperor. Father and Son shared the hint of a smile as the new Crown Prince was coronated with a crown worthy of the son and a son worthy of the crown.

Footnote

Kintsugi (or *Kintsukuroi*), which translates to "repair or rejoin with gold," is a Japanese art form of repairing broken pottery to emphasize vs. hide cracks and fractures with a special lacquer mixed with powdered gold. Just as the repaired ceramic becomes all the more beautiful for having been broken, these "scars of gold" are a metaphor that teaches us to see our brokenness as an opportunity to add beauty, strength, and character. Drawing from various *Kintsugi* origin stories, this is my retelling of the legend.

The technique dates back to the 15th century and aligns with the Japanese philosophy of *Wabi-Sabi. Wabi* refers to simplicity, humility, and living in tune with nature. At the same time, *Sabi* represents the passage of time and the acceptance of the natural cycle of growth, decay, and renewal. *Sabi* acknowledges the beauty that emerges as things weather and age.

Wabi-Sabi seeks intentionally and mindfully created experiences. It values authenticity and embraces the idea that beauty lies in the process, not just in the final result. It encourages a shift in perspective, inviting individuals to see the beauty in the ordinary, embrace the transient nature of existence, and cultivate contentment with what is rather than constantly striving for perfection or permanence.

The four pillars of manhood that the King teaches his son in the story (to reject passivity, to accept responsibility, to lead courageously, and to expect God's reward) are from the book *Raising a Modern Day Knight - A Father's Role in Guiding His Son to Authentic Manhood* (2007) by Dr. Robert Lewis. It played a central role in the philosophy I developed as a father to my son and daughter.

This ancient story of brokenness made beautiful is the perfect opening metaphor for a sabbatical. Just as *Kintsugi* turns fractures into strength, your sabbatical is the chance to repair and realign your own life with gold — reclaiming what I call sovereignty across mind, body, and spirit for a purposeful, more radiant second act.

Introduction

"What are you doing for you?"
- Glenn H.

My friend Glenn asked that question every time we met for breakfast. He could see that I was fried – and I knew it, too. Nearly three decades into a career that had shifted from energizing to exhausting, I was grinding through life's storms while family, mortgage, and a million other excuses kept me stuck on autopilot. His nudge lingered: *Wake up! Invest in yourself!*

A sabbatical is that kind of investment—a deliberate pivot for the state and the fate of your future self. It's a once-in-a-lifetime chance to turn off the autopilot and realign your trajectory.

The purpose of this book is to help you get the highest possible return on that investment. *Sabbaticaleer* walks with you to craft a custom strategy, grounded in a proven, proprietary filter, so you can build a sabbatical plan that pays long-term dividends. And it works whether you're just considering the idea, actively prepping, or already on your way.

This book is built with a natural rhythm: you do the work, then you step back and reflect. We alternate between hands-on workshop chapters that walk you step by step through building your personal sabbatical strategy and deeper "lessons learned" chapters drawn from my own 321-day experience.

The workshop chapters give you the "how."

The lessons-learned chapters give you the "what it feels like" — the bigger-picture wisdom that helps the plan come alive, shows you which mindsets actually stick, and lets you see what long-term renewal looks like in practice.

Together they create one seamless journey: you build, you reflect, you build some more — until you end up with both a solid plan and the clarity to live it.

Here's what you can expect from the workshop chapters:

Step 1 – Introduction to SPiCE — Gut check the current state of your five SPiCE pillars (Spiritual, Physical, Intellectual, Currencies - what you treasure, and Emotional) and then dig deeper to understand where you're strong and where you need shifts. This baseline grounds you in truth, not guesswork, to craft a custom plan with clear success metrics.

Step 2 – Purpose — Define your sabbatical's high-level purpose(s) by digging around in *Sabbaticaleer's* four primary sandboxes — *Exploration*, *Restoration*, *Growth*, and *Objective* — or *ERGO* for short. Explore them, rank them, pick your top two, and connect them to your SPiCE needs for a strategic foundation that sets you in the right direction.

Step 3 – Metrics and Self-Reflection — Create your living dashboard — journal, SWOT analysis (Strengths, Weaknesses, Opportunities, Threats), ongoing SPiCE snapshots — to track progress, catch shifts, and stay accountable like a boss on this exciting journey, not a tourist.

Step 4 – Best Practices — Reboot your head and heart with ten battle-tested best practices (starting with Be Authentic) to avoid pitfalls and align your trajectory for real success.

Step 5 – Time to Brainstorm your Sabbatical! — Dream big and write it all down — SPiCE goals for the shifts you *need*, ideas for the fun you *want* — then use the provided questionnaire to capture anchors and patterns.

Step 6 – Fulcrums — Filter your brainstorm into high-leverage *Fulcrums* — super-charged ideas that hit multiple SPiCE pillars at once — prioritizing what maximizes impact without spreading you thin.

Step 7 – Strategy Brief — Tie it all together into a 1–2 page living document — purpose, SPiCE goals, high-impact ideas (your fulcrums), itinerary, timing, and legacy — for a clear, measurable plan you can confidently execute and revisit.

Download the free *Sabbaticaleer Workbook* at sabbaticaleer.com.

The free workbook is the practical companion to the book *Sabbaticaleer: Your Best Job Ever - Build a Sabbatical That Lasts*. While the main book gives you the strategy, stories, and big ideas, the downloadable *Sabbaticaleer Workbook* PDF gives you the tools: clean printable worksheets, simple trackers, and quick-reference pages you can write on, mark up, and come back to again and again.

Think of your sabbatical as not just an important personal investment, but the most crucial rebranding campaign you'll ever run—because the brand is you. I learned from my career that a great rebrand starts with stripping away the old layers that no longer serve you, then rebuilding with intention: clearer purpose, sharper edges, and a story that excites. A sabbatical does that for your life—pausing the grind to realign your SPiCE pillars, ditch what's draining, and emerge renewed for a second act that's stronger, more authentic, and ready to shine. It's high-stakes work, but the return? A you that's not just surviving, but thriving like never before.

Because a sabbatical is a fundamentally introspective affair, here are a few questions to ponder before you proceed.

Do I need a Sabbatical or just a great Vacation?

The word "sabbatical" traces back to the Greek *sabbaton* and Hebrew *shabbāth*—both meaning rest. In the biblical sense, to rest is to dwell in peace when life is placed back in right order. It echoes God's seventh-day pause in Genesis after creation and the fallow year in Leviticus, when the land itself was given time to renew.

A successful sabbatical aspires to do the same for you: to realign your life with a deep sense of peace and restore it to its proper order.

This isn't an open-ended vacation; it's a purposeful reset and realignment. As I said, my own lasted 321 days—about ten and a half months. Yours could be shorter or longer. Some companies may offer weeks or months of sabbatical leave after years of service; most are self-funded. For this book and our purposes, a sabbatical is defined as follows:

<u>sab*bat*i*cal:</u> *A defined period of intentionally focused activity and renewal, resulting in a purposeful, personal realignment for successful second acts of life.*

Vacation recharges batteries. Sabbatical rewrites the operating system and shapes the legacy you leave. Vacations let you flee reality; sabbaticals require you to face it, often uncomfortably, for change that sticks. Ready to tell the difference?

Sabbatical	Vacation
Renewal & Realignment	Recovery & Escape
Self-Refleciton Required	Self-Reflection Optional
Activities & Growth-Focused	Activities-Focused
Interests and Outcomes Oriented	Interests Oriented
Long-Term Implications	Short-Term Implications
Paradigm-Shifting	Stress-Relieving
Legacy Influencing	Not Legacy Influencing

What are you doing for you?

Sabbaticaleer is here to ask you the same question Glenn asked me. What are you doing for you? And are you ready to do more? And why now? Something's stirring. Is the sand shifting below your feet, and you're seeking solid ground? Maybe burnout's got you running on fumes, or loss has shaken your foundation, or you're rich on paper but hollow inside. Maybe its time for you to get that thing done you've been dreaming of. Maybe you're just hungry for hope and a life that feels like yours again in an increasingly disorienting world changing at breakneck speed. For me, it was a handful of things that I will touch on later that left me circling the drain and needing change.

You're not alone.

Designer Stefan Sagmeister famously shuts his studio every seven years for a full-year sabbatical — Bali hikes, experiments in happiness and beauty — and credits those breaks with some of his best creative work.

A 57-year-old engineer left his corporate job to rejoin the Peace Corps for three years, later calling it career- and life-saving: "My soul was drowning in stuff." Another took time to trace family roots in South America and returned engaged and clearer-headed.

These aren't outliers. They're proof that the long game works.

You've picked up this book because you're considering a sabbatical, intrigued by the idea, or maybe have one in the works. *Sabbaticaleer* wants to help you make it a reality.

There are no age requirements for sabbaticals, though a mindset shift is required. This book isn't about escaping life; it's about rewriting the map. We'll navigate the fears that hold you back, unlock the goals that ignite your soul, and craft a sabbatical plan that rewrites your narrative from "What has become of me?" to "Who will I become next?" We'll follow a blueprint for personal excavation and align your compass for rediscovering your most vibrant self.

Are you ready?

Everybody enters their sabbatical on their own timeline, based on their own circumstances. Maybe you've already decided to take one, or you're just seriously considering it. Maybe you've already started and need a little guidance to get the most out of it. The more prep work and thinking you do in advance, the better you'll be able to maximize the precious, finite days, weeks, and months of your sabbatical.

If that quiet voice inside you is whispering, or shouting...listen.

Grab a notebook, jot down why you're here right now. This book pays it forward: best practices, tools, and hard-won lessons so you can craft a successful sabbatical that's yours alone.

Let's get to work - Your best job ever starts with Chapter 1

How the Book Works – Your Journey Through *Sabbaticaleer*

Here's how the book is structured to give you exactly what you need. We alternate between the hands-on workshop chapters that walk you step by step through building your personal sabbatical strategy and deeper "lessons learned" chapters drawn from my own 321-day experience and a career in advertising and brand-building. The workshop chapters give you the practical "how." The lessons chapters give you the "what it feels like" and the bigger-picture wisdom that make the plan come alive. Together they create one seamless journey: you build, you reflect, you build some more — until you end up with both a solid plan and the clarity to live it.

Here's how the chapters unfold:

Sabbaticaleer – An Alternating Work / Think Flow

Chapter 1: The SPiCE of Your Life (Work – Baseline Assessment) – Discover SPiCE — your personal dashboard for the five core pillars of well-being — and get an honest baseline reading on where you stand today and tomorrow.

Chapter 2: Knowledge vs Narrative (Think – Questioning the Stories) – Question the stories and assumptions that have been quietly shaping your life. Learn to spot the machinery behind them and start reclaiming cognitive sovereignty over your own mind.

Chapter 3: Define Your Purpose – Aim High from Solid Ground (Work – High-Level Purpose) – Choose your sabbatical's high-level purpose from the four ERGO sandboxes (Exploration, Restoration, Growth & Objective) and connect it to your SPiCE needs so you have a clear strategic foundation.

Chapter 4: Image vs Identity (Think – Who You Really Are) – Look honestly at the gap between the image you project to the world and the identity you actually carry inside, and learn how to align the two so you can live more authentically.

Chapter 5: Self-Reflection & Metrics (Work – Building Your Dashboard) – Create your living dashboard — journal, SWOT analysis (**S**trengths, **W**eaknesses, **O**pportunities & **T**hreats) and ongoing SPiCE snapshots — so you can track progress, catch shifts, and stay accountable like the CEO of your own sabbatical.

Chapter 6: Ancient System, Modern Wisdom (Think – A Practical System That Works) – Discover the ancient system that strengthened all five of my SPiCE pillars at once and became one of the most powerful tools of my entire sabbatical. Yoga was the practice I found that worked powerfully for me. While I'm a strong advocate, the real gift of a sabbatical is finding what works for you. For me, yoga had the rare quality of touching all five pillars simultaneously — and it can become a simple, repeatable practice that delivers lasting sovereignty over your mind, body, and spirit long after the sabbatical ends.

Chapter 7: Best Practices to Reset Your Mindset (Work – Mindset Reboot) – Reboot your head and heart with ten battle-tested best practices (starting with "Be Authentic") to avoid common pitfalls and align your trajectory for real success.

Chapter 8: Systems That Stick (Think – Turning Insights into Routines) – Turn sabbatical insights into everyday routines and rituals you can maintain long after the official time off ends. Learn how small, repeatable systems quietly compound into lasting change and real sovereignty across every SPiCE pillar.

Chapter 9: Time to Brainstorm your Sabbatical! (Work – Generating Ideas) – Dream big and capture everything you both *need* and *want* from your sabbatical — SPiCE goals for the shifts you need and ideas for the experiences that light you up.

Chapter 10: A Sabbatical that Lasts (Think – Real-World Proof) – See what long-term renewal actually looks like years after the official sabbatical ends. Discover how the systems you build during your time off — including the Wabi-Sabi lessons from restoring my 1970 Pagoda — can quietly keep paying dividends for the rest of your life.

Chapter 11: Filter Your Fulcrums (Work – Prioritizing Impact) – Filter your brainstorm into high-leverage fulcrums — the powerful ideas that hit multiple SPiCE pillars at once — so you can maximize impact without spreading yourself thin.

Chapter 12: Envisioning Your Second Act with Legacy in Mind (Think – The Bigger Why) – Step back from the tactical work and paint a vivid picture of the life you want to live. Explore how to move from SPiCE goals and fulcrums to a clear, inspiring vision of your days, relationships, contributions, and the legacy you hope to leave — so your sabbatical becomes the bridge to a truly meaningful second act.

Chapter 13: Assembling Your Sabbatical Strategy Brief (Work – Final Plan) – Pull everything together into a clear, one-to-two-page living document that becomes your personal roadmap for a successful sabbatical.

Chapter 14: The World Needs More Heroes (Think – Legacy and Paying It Forward) – Lift your eyes outward to legacy and the idea that your realigned life can quietly become heroic for others. Explore how the inner work of a sabbatical can ripple outward in meaningful ways.

Epilogue: Your Best Job Ever Is Just Getting Started – Realize that a sabbatical is not a temporary reset or a vacation — it is the most important job you'll ever take on: the work of putting your life back in proper order. Carry the systems, sovereignty, and SPiCE alignment you built into the second half of your life as an ongoing operating system, so the real second act keeps compounding long after the official time off ends.

Chapter One

The SPiCE of Your Life

"In this time, the most precious substance in the universe is the Spice...The Spice extends life. The Spice extends consciousness."
— Frank Herbert, *Dune*

Frank Herbert built an entire universe around *Spice* — the rare substance that fuels travel, sharpens awareness, and extends life itself. We don't have interstellar melange, but we've got our own SPiCE — closer to home, brewed from the essential ingredients of a life worth living.

This chapter introduces you to the *Sabbaticaleer* SPiCE filter — five core pillars that make up your personal ecosystem. Get clear on where you're strong, where you're running low, and what needs tending, and suddenly your sabbatical stops being a vague escape. It becomes a deliberate reset, the pivot to a strategic second act tuned to who you really are and what you actually need.

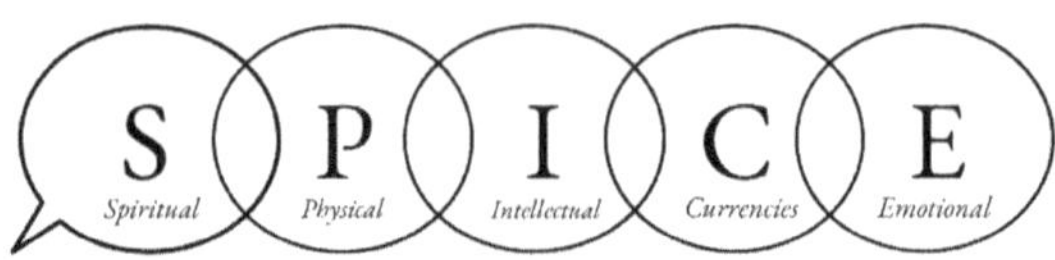

• **S** is for **Spiritual** — the inner spark. Reconnecting your spirit with purpose, values, that quiet hum of meaning that keeps you pointed true north, whether through faith, awe, or honest self-reflection.

• **P** is for **Physical** — your vibrant vessel. Honoring the body that carries you: strength, energy, resilience, navigating the grind before it demands more than it's worth.

• **I** is for **Intellectual** — your curious mind. Feeding the hunger for new ideas, challenging old views, igniting lifelong learning that keeps the brain sharp and adaptable.

• **C** is for **Currencies** — the treasures you value. Beyond finances: relationships, experiences, and qualities that make you feel genuinely rich and fulfilled.

• **E** is for **Emotional** — your well-being. Navigating feelings with grace, building peace, and developing the resilience to bounce back stronger, rather than breaking.

Nurture these five, and they don't just sit there — they interact. Think of it like a good stew: each ingredient strengthens the overall flavor. A fed spirit bolsters emotional steadiness and even physical health. A strong body sharpens thinking and extends vitality. Lifelong learning keeps you nimble and fulfilled. Honoring what you truly value steers you toward purpose. Emotional balance lets you ride life's waves without capsizing.

It's an old idea dressed in new clothes. Hippocrates saw healing as holistic — body, mind, spirit, environment, all tangled together. Twenty-four centuries later, modern research echoes him. The pillars reinforce each other in a symphony of well-being.

So as you step into this sabbatical, you're not reinventing the wheel. You're tapping ancient wisdom about interconnectedness and weaving your own thread into a tapestry that's been building for millennia.

When you pause intentionally and filter your priorities through your SPiCE, the return isn't just recovery — it's reinvention.

Ready to dig in? Grab your journal (we'll lean on it hard in later chapters). Let's walk through the pillars one by one, spot potential cues, and start to understand what a truly tailored sabbatical looks like for you.

Spiritual

The why beneath the what. That tug in your chest when something feels holy, bigger than you. Reconnecting with purpose, values, and the quiet hum of meaning — through faith, awe, or plain self-honesty.

Ask yourself: When did you last feel aligned with something larger than daily tasks? What stirs awe or wonder in you? Are you living a life that feels meaningful, or just busy?

When nurtured, this pillar becomes a compass — decisions feel grounded, life has direction. When ignored, days feel empty, motivation drifts, and the other pillars lose their anchor.

Physical

How alive your living, breathing body actually feels. The raw engine of sweat, sleep, sunlight, and sensation. Honoring the vessel that carries you: building strength, vitality, and resilience so your body can better serve your dreams and minimize the handcuffs of the pharmaceutical hamster wheel.

Ask yourself: Do you wake up feeling rested or dragged? When did your body last feel capable and light instead of heavy? What small daily habits would help you gain more energy?

When nurtured, energy flows naturally, movement feels good, and sleep restores. When ignored, fatigue becomes chronic, pain creeps in, and the whole system slows.

Intellectual

The brain's playtime. Not the daily work grind; wild learning that makes your eyebrows raise. Feeding curiosity, challenging old views, igniting lifelong sparks that keep you adaptable and sharp.

Ask yourself: When was the last time a new idea genuinely excited you? Has learning started to feel like a chore? What question have you been avoiding because it might change how you see things?

When nurtured, ideas spark, perspectives widen, and adaptability grows. When ignored, mental fog settles, creativity stalls, and life feels repetitive.

Currencies

Whatever you choose to measure life by. Could be hours with kids, unread books stacked high, miles walked in silence. Yours to mint: relationships, experiences, qualities that make you feel genuinely rich and full.

Ask yourself: What makes you feel truly wealthy — time, connection, freedom? Are you trading life for the wrong currencies? What would abundance look like on your terms?

When nurtured, time feels plentiful, relationships deepen, and experiences accumulate. When ignored, emptiness grows even when the bank account is full.

Emotional

Letting the weather inside you move. Tears, laughter, rage, tenderness — clean air for the heart. Building inner steadiness and resilience so you can navigate the full spectrum with grace, bend without breaking, and bounce back stronger.

Ask yourself: Do emotions flow freely or get stuck? When did you last feel peace instead of constant tension? How do you handle the hard feelings — numb them or let them pass? How resilient are you when life throws a curve?

When nurtured, resilience becomes natural, and peace settles in. When ignored, storms linger, numbness creeps in, and everything feels heavier.

Your Gut-Check SPiCE Baseline

Any serious endeavor — whether launching a business, training for a marathon, or building a life worth living — requires honest measurement. You can't improve what you don't track.

So grab a pen or pencil and let's rate where you think you stand right now across each of your five SPiCE pillars. This is just a high-level, gut-check. Don't overthink it. First impressions are valuable data. Later we'll dig deeper, but for now we'll keep it simple. Rate yourself 1-10 across your five pillars. The scale is divided into three zones: Thriving (8-10), Surviving (4-7) or Dying (1-3).

- **Thriving** means you're feeling healthy here, energized, flowing (Your dashboard lights are Green)

- **Surviving** means things are marginal, you're getting by, but no real vitality (Dashboard lights are flashing Yellow)

- **Dying** means levels are critically low; you're drained to the point things may feel unsustainable (Dashboard is lights flashing Red)

Circle the number that best represents where you stand today – mark the date. For an extra level of metrics sophistication, add a directional arrow to each: is it on the rise, declining, or holding steady?

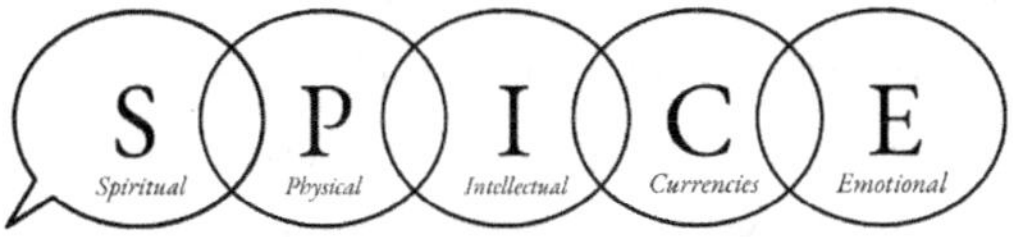

	S *Spiritual*	P *Physical*	I *Intellectual*	C *Currencies*	E *Emotional*
	10	10	10	10	10
Thriving	9	9	9	9	9
	8	8	8	8	8
	7	7	7	7	7
Surviving	6	6	6	6	6
	5	5	5	5	5
	4	4	4	4	4
	3	3	3	3	3
Dying	2	2	2	2	2
	1	1	1	1	1

This is your first **Pre-Sabbatical baseline**. It's not judgment — it's data. When you're on sabbatical, you'll track it regularly so you can see progress, plateaus, or new gaps. Later we'll expand this into full metrics and journaling practices, but for now this quick scan gives you a starting point and a personal frame of reference as we dig deeper into each of the pillars

Deeper Dive: Spiritual – The Inner Spark

Catalysts in the Spiritual pillar often arrive as a quiet void: days that may be full but leave you feeling empty, a nagging sense that life is just busy without meaning, or a crisis that shakes your values to the core. These aren't random — they're signals that the daily grind has dulled your inner spark, disconnecting you from awe, faith, or honest self-reflection.

Socrates gave us the battle cry of the examined life, Aristotle built on it with *eudaimonia* as a lifelong pursuit of virtue and meaning, Okinawa's centenarians show us the quiet power of *ikigai* – their simple reason for being, Mark's Gospel invites a profound change of heart and mind through *metanoia*, and Hippocrates reminded us that true balance includes the spirit within the whole person. In your Spiritual pillar, these ancient voices converge around one central question:

Am I living in alignment with what truly matters?

Socrates would call this the examined life. He famously said the unexamined life is not worth living and that "know thyself" is the starting point of all wisdom. A sabbatical gives you the rare space to do this deep work without distraction — to look honestly at your inner compass and decide which direction feels true.

Research backs the ancient wisdom. A strong spiritual practice correlates with lower depression, anxiety, and substance abuse, plus higher resilience and well-being.

A sabbatical becomes a "leap of faith" here: you step out of the grind to realign, engaging both secular and sacred. DJ DiDonna felt that void after career burnout. He walked 900 miles on Japan's Shikoku pilgrimage — a slow, deliberate path that reignited his sense of purpose and led him to found *The Sabbatical Project.*

So lean into that tug in your chest. Your sabbatical is the space to aim high, maybe miss the mark sometimes, and realign without judgment. Feed this spark, and watch how it lights up the rest of your SPiCE.

Deeper Dive: Physical – The Raw Engine

Chronic exhaustion that no weekend fixes. A health scare that stops you cold. Persistent pain, weight creep, or a body running on fumes while the mind keeps pushing. These are loud physical catalysts — signals that the daily grind has outpaced your physiology.

Socrates urged us to examine the body as part of the examined life, Aristotle saw physical excellence as part of *eudaimonia*, Okinawa's *ikigai* keeps people active and purposeful into their 100s, Mark's *metanoia* calls for turning away from habits that harm us, and Hippocrates placed the body at the center of his holistic view of healing and balance. In your Physical pillar, these ideas remind us that the body is not separate from the rest of life — it is the vessel through which everything else is lived.

Hippocrates, the father of medicine, saw the body as part of a larger whole. He taught that true health comes from balance — not just treating symptoms but supporting the body's natural ability to heal through diet, movement, rest, and harmony with your environment. Your Physical pillar is asking:

Am I giving my body the daily conditions it needs to thrive, or am I outsourcing its care to quick fixes and constant busyness?

A sabbatical is the perfect time to rebuild that balance from the inside out. On your sabbatical, this pillar gets practical fast. Rebuild sleep debt. Move in ways that feel good. Eat real food that fuels, not numbs. Let sunlight and fresh air do their quiet work. The goal isn't vanity — it's vitality.

Sonia, a public health expert, hit burnout and grief after years of high-stakes work. Her three-month sabbatical prioritized deep rest, gentle movement, real nourishment, and time with loved ones. She emerged with sustained energy and a clearer sense of what sustains her physically.

What's your body asking for right now? Your sabbatical is the chance to listen — and answer — with action.

Deeper Dive: Intellectual – The Brain's Playtime

Mental fog, ideas that used to excite now feel flat, conversations loop without depth. Burnout's intellectual toll — stagnation, reduced focus, lost creativity — is a clear signal it's time to pause.

Socrates taught that wisdom begins with admitting what we don't know, Aristotle defined the highest good as *eudaimonia* through reason and virtue, *ikigai* keeps the mind engaged through purposeful activity, Mark's *metanoia* invites a fundamental change in how we think, and Hippocrates saw intellectual clarity as inseparable from physical and environmental health. In your Intellectual pillar, these traditions all point toward the same invitation: to keep learning, questioning, and growing rather than settling into autopilot.

Aristotle built on Socrates with *eudaimonia* — a journey of constant moral and intellectual improvement through virtue, reason, meaningful activity, and relationships. In your Intellectual pillar, this invites the question:

Am I feeding my curiosity and growing in wisdom, or have I let my mind go on autopilot?

A sabbatical creates the space to rediscover the joy of learning for its own sake and to use your mind in ways that feel alive and purposeful. On your sabbatical, let the brain roam. Dive into unread books, take a class that intrigues you, explore a new skill without pressure.

The aim isn't instant expertise — it's reigniting the spark.

Deeper Dive: Currencies – Yours to Mint

Emptiness amid abundance, relationships strained from neglect, passions sidelined for work. These are catalysts that ask:

"What am I trading my life for?"

Socrates valued relationships as part of the examined life, Aristotle included meaningful friendships in *eudaimonia*, Okinawa's *ikigai* is rooted in community and contribution, Mark's *metanoia* calls for turning toward deeper connections, and Hippocrates recognized that social and environmental context shape our well-being. In your Currencies pillar, these ideas remind us that true wealth is measured not just in time or resources, but in the quality of our relationships and the sense of purpose we find through them.

In Okinawa, *ikigai* — "a reason for being" is woven into the fabric of society. It's a backstop that lifts up their senior citizens in a way our modern society lacks and that we must address individually. It's the quiet sense of purpose that comes from small, meaningful contributions, deep relationships, and feeling needed in your community. Your Currencies pillar asks:

What makes my days feel worth waking up for, and who and what am I investing my time and energy in?

A sabbatical gives you the breathing room to realign your relationships, time, and contributions around what truly matters.

During your sabbatical, mint deliberately. Reconnect with family without rush. Dive into that pile of unread books. Volunteer, travel lightly, build habits that prioritize what fills you.

During my own sabbatical I shifted boundaries to open myself up. I intentionally stopped wearing a watch to redefine time on my own terms. Instead of limiting time invested in new interactions, I let them unfold at their own pace.

Inventory your treasures. What's stacking up that doesn't fill you? Your sabbatical is the forge — mint what matters.

Deeper Dive: Emotional – Clean Air for the Heart

Inner turbulence: anxiety that won't settle, numbness masking grief, outbursts from unprocessed stress. Burnout's emotional fallout is a call to pause before the storm capsizes the rest.

Socrates saw emotional honesty as essential to self-knowledge, Aristotle understood that virtue includes steady emotional balance, *ikigai* brings calm through purpose and connection, *metanoia* is fundamentally an emotional turning of the heart, and Hippocrates recognized that emotional states affect physical health and vice versa. In your Emotional pillar, these traditions all speak to the same need: to move from reactivity toward greater steadiness, openness, and resilience.

Mark's *metanoia* calls for a radical heart-and-mind shift. *Metanoia* is actually the very first word Jesus speaks in the Gospel of Mark, translated as "Change your mind!" in the original Greek — far deeper and more powerful than the modern translation "repent," which is an expression of regret.

This is a complete turning around of your thinking, your priorities, and your direction of life. In your Emotional pillar, this is the gentle but powerful invitation to let go of old fears, resentments, or habits so you can live with greater steadiness and openness. A sabbatical offers the space for this kind of profound, lasting turning.

Emotional intelligence research links self-awareness and regulation to lower depression and higher resilience. Sabbaticals help heal this: intentional breaks reduce chronic stress.

In sabbatical practice, let emotions breathe. Journal your internal weather systems, seek therapy without shame, practice mindfulness. Build habits like walks or talks that clear the air.

Gordon MacDonald captures this long-game truth in *A Resilient Life*:

"It makes little difference how fast you can run the hundred meters when the race is 400 meters long. Life is not a sprint. It is a distance run, and it demands the kind of conditioning that enables people to go the distance."

Feel the weather shift. Your sabbatical is the clearing — let it move, build resilience, and breathe in the clean air that follows.

What a realigned and renewed you can look like

SPiCE is your living dashboard. It's your fuel gauge for spotting cues, assessing where you're thin, and building a sabbatical that's truly yours — no cookie-cutter plans, just truth tailored to your life.

What success can look like on the other side:

• **Spiritual** — A quiet, steady sense of alignment. Decisions flow from a deeper "why." Life feels meaningful, not just busy.

• **Physical** — Your body feels alive and capable again. Energy rooted in sound sleep, movement that feels good, sunlight on skin. Vitality returns.

• **Intellectual** — Curiosity reignited. Learning is play that lights you up. Ideas spark, perspectives shift, mind feels expansive.

• **Currencies**— Wealth redefined on your terms. Time with loved ones is abundant, experiences stack up that money can't buy, relationships are deepened.

• **Emotional** — Inner weather moves freely. You feel joy, grief, anger, tenderness — and process with grace. Resilience built-in. Peace as clean air after a long rain.

These aren't distant ideals. They're the real payoff waiting when you read the filter honestly and start acting on what it reveals.

The single most important thing you can do right now is get an honest baseline reading on your SPiCE levels. Over the next five pages you'll find five focused questions for each pillar. They'll help you move beyond your initial gut check and create a clear, dimensionalized score for where you stand today.

Sabbaticaleer strongly encourages you to complete the questionnaire while the chapter is still fresh. Take a few quiet minutes, be candid, and jot any insights that surface. These baseline scores will become your most valuable reference point as you build your custom strategy — and the foundation you'll pivot from for the long haul of your second act.

You're at the beginning of an exciting journey!

SPiCE – Spiritual

Purpose:

Do your mornings greet you with a clear sense of purpose?

0 — 1 — 2 — 3 — 4 — 5 — 6 — 7 — 8 — 9 — 10

Compass:

Can you still hear and trust your inner compass?

0 — 1 — 2 — 3 — 4 — 5 — 6 — 7 — 8 — 9 — 10

Faith:

How strong is your faith—divine, gut, or grit?

0 — 1 — 2 — 3 — 4 — 5 — 6 — 7 — 8 — 9 — 10

Connection:

Do you feel part of something larger and meaningful?

0 — 1 — 2 — 3 — 4 — 5 — 6 — 7 — 8 — 9 — 10

Gratitude:

How deeply do you feel and express gratitude each day?

0 — 1 — 2 — 3 — 4 — 5 — 6 — 7 — 8 — 9 — 10

Total / Divide by 5 → Spiritual Score: ________

Observations & Insights

---

0 - 3 = Dying, critical • 4 - 7=-Surviving, marginal • 8 -10 = Thriving, strong

Circle one number per question, then total each pillar and divide by 5 for your average score.

SPiCE – Intellectual

Spark

Did anything new spark real curiosity or excitement in your mind last week?

0 — 1 — 2 — 3 — 4 — 5 — 6 — 7 — 8 — 9 — 10

Curiosity

Is your mind hungry for new ideas, or half-closed?

0 — 1 — 2 — 3 — 4 — 5 — 6 — 7 — 8 — 9 — 10

Ideas

Do new ideas still excite and energize you?

0 — 1 — 2 — 3 — 4 — 5 — 6 — 7 — 8 — 9 — 10

Depth

Are your conversations and thinking deep, or mostly surface-level?

0 — 1 — 2 — 3 — 4 — 5 — 6 — 7 — 8 — 9 — 10

Adaptability

Do new challenges sharpen your thinking and open new possibilities?

0 — 1 — 2 — 3 — 4 — 5 — 6 — 7 — 8 — 9 — 10

Total / Divide by 5 → Intellectual Score: __

Observations & Insights

---

0 - 3 = Dying, critical • 4 - 7=-Surviving, marginal • 8 -10 = Thriving, strong

Circle one number per question, then total each pillar and divide by 5 for your average score.

SPiCE – Currencies

Security

Do you feel secure with your time, money, and resources?

0 — 1 — 2 — 3 — 4 — 5 — 6 — 7 — 8 — 9 — 10

Ownership

Do you own your hours, or do they own you?

0 — 1 — 2 — 3 — 4 — 5 — 6 — 7 — 8 — 9 — 10

Relationships

Are your relationships rich and nourishing, or ragged?

0 — 1 — 2 — 3 — 4 — 5 — 6 — 7 — 8 — 9 — 10

Growth

Are your skills and experiences growing, or gathering dust?

0 — 1 — 2 — 3 — 4 — 5 — 6 — 7 — 8 — 9 — 10

Legacy

Is your impact building steadily in ways that matter to you?

0 — 1 — 2 — 3 — 4 — 5 — 6 — 7 — 8 — 9 — 10

Total / Divide by 5 → Currencies Score: ________

Observations & Insights

---

0 - 3 = Dying, critical • 4 - 7=-Surviving, marginal • 8 -10 = Thriving, strong

Circle one number per question, then total each pillar and divide by 5 for your average score.

SPiCE – Emotional

Openness

Is your heart open and free, or locked tight?

0 — 1 — 2 — 3 — 4 — 5 — 6 — 7 — 8 — 9 — 10

Joy

Does joy feel abundant or scarce?

0 — 1 — 2 — 3 — 4 — 5 — 6 — 7 — 8 — 9 — 10

Peace

Do you carry an inner peace, even when life is stormy?

0 — 1 — 2 — 3 — 4 — 5 — 6 — 7 — 8 — 9 — 10

Tears

Do tears come when they should, without shame?

0 — 1 — 2 — 3 — 4 — 5 — 6 — 7 — 8 — 9 — 10

Love

Is love moving freely in and out of your life?

0 — 1 — 2 — 3 — 4 — 5 — 6 — 7 — 8 — 9 — 10

Total / Divide by 5 → Emotional Score: ________

Observations & Insights

---

0 - 3 = Dying, critical • 4 - 7=-Surviving, marginal • 8 -10 = Thriving, strong

Circle one number per question, then total each pillar and divide by 5 for your average score.

Your Homework

After you fill out the questionnaire and calculate your baseline SPiCE scores, fill out the table below with your initial gut-check scores from earlier in the chapter along with your updated scores.

Carry this over to your journal for continuity and write down any insights, shifts or surprises you encountered.

Make note of the pillars that need the most attention and which questions sparked deeper questions for you as you begin to look ahead.

SPiCE Pillar	Initial Gut Score	Follow up Worksheet Score	Note Dates/Insights/Shifts
Spiritual			
Physical			
Intellectual			
Currencies			
Emotional			

Chapter Two

Knowledge vs Narrative

"Those who tell the stories rule the world."
— Anonymous

Assumption is a fascinating word. On one hand, it means something we accept as true without proof. On the other, it means taking on power or responsibility. It's the perfect sabbatical word.

A sabbatical gives you the rare chance to step back from the daily grind and challenge every assumption you've been carrying — especially after you've just taken that honest SPiCE snapshot in the last chapter. It's a time to look at your life objectively — and then decide which skin you want to shed and which new one you want to step into. It's also the moment you take on new power and new responsibilities for the second act you actually want to live.

That's why sabbatical is such a formidable forcing function. It's an intentional pause that shifts your behaviors and your mindset so you can build a more satisfying, more successful life. Socrates nailed it back in Chapter 1: "The unexamined life is not worth living." He wasn't debating whether life has value —

he was challenging us to use self-reflection and critical thinking to create one that does.

The Workshop chapters of this book walk you through checking your SPiCE levels and building your Strategy Brief. Whether you're knee-deep in your sabbatical right now or still planning it, the alternating chapters intentionally shift the focus. Here we challenge assumptions, encourage real self-reflection, and break free of the confirmation bias that keeps so many of us chained in the dark.

The Ad-Man's Confession

I spent almost thirty years in advertising helping craft narratives that moved product and shaped perceptions. On a strategic level, we called it "positioning." The client wanted you to believe their toothpaste would make you irresistible, their cancer stick would make you a rugged individualist, or — in one memorable case from my own adventures — that their fat-free cheese would melt and stretch like the real thing.

Proof of concept was supposed to be delivered in a shot called "the cheese pull." You've seen it a thousand times: a hot slice lifting away from the pizza, strings of gooey cheese stretching forever. Except this stuff didn't pull. It curled up like burnt cardboard in the oven. Network TV regulations required actual product use always, but no problem — we fired up a wardrobe steamer, blasted that cheese until it behaved, slid it in to cook, and... *voila*. Perfect cheese pull. Fair to say your initial purchase could safely *assume* quality performance and taste – and you would be wrong.

Everything was tested — headlines, images, every click measured for persuasiveness. All to find the narrow levers and slivers of truth that could be leveraged to create motivating narratives. The longer I did it, the more I saw how the same tricks get used on all of us: by politicians, influencers, even our own inner voice. And I started to wonder: if I could spot the machinery in advertising so easily, how many other narratives was I naively swallowing across other aspects of life?

Sabbatical gave me the time and distance to turn that priority inward and begin auditing the stories I'd been buying myself for decades.

The One Sentence That Changed Everything

Then there was a little eye-opening episode at the office. A well-known Creative Director at our agency wrote a column for a trade publication bemoaning brands being "addicted to promotion." He used his own personal struggles with drug addiction as his metaphorical hook. He sent it out without running it by anyone. It caused an absolute uproar. Clients were furious – not just about the reference, but the implication that they were small minded due to this "addiction." The agency scrambled. And in that moment it hit me: every message you consume — every story, every opinion, every headline — is controlled, ultimately bought and paid for by somebody, somewhere up some ladder.

I wrote that realization on an index card and carried it in my pocket for months. Three simple words to apply to an experiment and personal litmus test: "Who, What, and Why?" Whenever I was witness to or felt myself getting pulled into a narrative, I asked: Who's behind this? What exact message are they pushing? And why — what's the real agenda? I rarely got clean answers, and that was the point. The power wasn't in understanding every detail; it was in realizing there is almost always a "who" with money and motive pulling the strings, a "what" they want you to believe, and a "why" that serves them. The truth is, I'm still pulled into narratives that seek to manipulate. But those three questions — Who, What, and Why — became the mantra that began to crack open my own little corner of the cave we're all trapped in.

Over time that moment became an early catalyst for something I've come to call *Cognitive Sovereignty* — the personal right (and responsibility) and regular practice of independently evaluating information, questioning dominant narratives, and maintaining mental independence from external influences, algorithms, or paid agendas. It's not a term I coined; but it's a concept that has taken shape for me throughout my whole life and career. It's one that humankind has always faced - usually without even knowing or caring that we are: from the king's town crier telling the village what they *need to know*, to the era of the Big Three network's Evening News telling America, to today's quickly morphing digital and AI driven narrative reality.

Acknowledging the role of cognitive sovereignty captures what is at risk today if we ignore the forces at play. The advent of AI has turbocharged both the promise and the peril. Algorithms already knew how to keep us hooked; now they can generate personalized narratives faster than any human can fact-check them. AI doesn't just reflect our biases — it can anticipate them, amplify them, and serve them back before we've finished our coffee. The feed stays one step ahead, happy to stoke our confirmation biases and take us where it wants us to go. Ask yourself:

Where does it want to take us collectively and you personally? What's the motivation at play?

It's fair to say it's not the truth it pushes, or unity, or joy.

Sabbatical gives us the room to explore and question the narratives we may allowing ourselves to embrace (and negatively influence us) absent-mindedly. Shoring up your cognitive sovereignty isn't optional anymore if you seek to pro-actively take or regain authorship of your life.

Narrative Traps We Fall Into After 40

By the time we hit mid-life, too often too many of us are carrying around a heavy load of other people's expectations. We try to live up to what our parents wanted, our kids need, our colleagues expect, and even what society says a "successful" second act should look like. The problem is those expectations are moving targets, and chasing them is exhausting.

Expectations, by definition, are not rooted in reality. Instead, they are untethered products and projections of the mind. "Premeditated resentments" is what my Ph.D. therapist and friend Andy Ward aptly calls expectations—the bitter pill we create for ourselves. By contrast, an ongoing process of self-reflection empowers us to live authentically, equipping us to navigate life with resilience, emotional stability, and purpose, and represents the foundation of true wisdom.

I've learned that gratitude is the secret to happiness and expectations are the road to misery. You can never fully meet other people's expectations because they're always shifting. But you can choose gratitude instead of envy or anger every single day. It's lighter. It's freer. And it's one of the simplest ways to start rewriting your own narrative on your own terms.

Once you start noticing how many of those second-hand expectations you've been living inside, another older story becomes hard to ignore — the one about the prisoners and the shadows on the wall.

The Cave, the Algorithm, and the Mirror

Plato described it perfectly more than 2,400 years ago in his *Allegory of the Cave*. Prisoners chained in a dark cave are manipulated by unseen puppeteers to see only shadows cast on the wall by a fire behind them. They believe those shadows are reality. When one prisoner escapes, climbs into the sunlight, and sees the real world, he can barely believe it. When he returns to tell the others, they think he's crazy. They prefer the comfort of the shadows they know.

This theme has echoed throughout history as a moving target describing the human condition. From Plato in ancient Greece, through George Orwell's *1984* with its Ministry of Truth rewriting reality on demand, to the Wachowskis' *The Matrix* — where humans live plugged into a simulated world while their bodies are enslaved and harvested for energy — the cave keeps reappearing in new forms. The shadows are intentionally designed to keep us comfortable and compliant. Spotting them and climbing out is the ongoing challenge that Socrates described as the downfall of the "unexamined life."

That allegory has never been more relevant. Today the fire is the algorithms, and the shadows are the endless feed on the screens designed to keep us engaged, outraged, or reassured. The moving target is always there, intentionally or not, challenging us to see clearly.

A sabbatical is the rare stretch (if you're disciplined) where you can unplug from the grid and the grind and let the mirror — not the matrix — tell you who you actually are. It's your deliberate escape from the cave, the chance to see clearly before deciding which parts of the old narrative you want to bring back with you.

When Knowledge Hits Home

Breakthroughs are inevitably triggered by encounters with a topic or situation in the media where you have specific expertise or firsthand knowledge, and the media narrative conflicts with what you know to be true. For the thoughtful few, that disconnect becomes the first step out of the cave. For most, unfortunately, it's easier to shrug and keep watching the shadows.

Most people never take that escape. The ones who do usually start with a single, uncomfortable moment of recognition.

Perception vs Perspective

The first real crack in the cave often arrives the same way: you run into a story or claim that collides with something you know to be true from your own experience. That collision is useful — but only if you notice how you're looking at it.

Perception is how something first lands with you in the moment — the immediate, often automatic interpretation shaped by your senses, emotions, biases, and past experiences. It's raw and highly subjective. Perspective is the wider lens you deliberately choose to look through, guided by your values, new insights, and conscious reflection. Perception happens to you. Perspective is something you can step back and change.

Whether you are currently on sabbatical or not, your SPiCE pillars give you a practical way to develop better perspective, especially if — like most of us — you've been running parts of your life on autopilot. Autopilot shows up differently across every pillar, and it almost always begins as perception — that fast, unexamined reaction we barely notice.

Spiritual autopilot might look like going through the motions of faith or purpose without ever asking if the story still fits.

Physical autopilot might look like keeping the body driving on the same fuel and schedule even when the warning lights are flashing.

Intellectual autopilot might look like defending a comfortable set of opinions without testing them.

Currencies autopilot might look like running the same money and relationship patterns because "that's just how it's always been."

Emotional autopilot might look like letting the old trigger fire the same response every time.

In each case, perception hands us the first automatic version of the story. Perspective is the deliberate pause that lets us decide whether that story still belongs to the life we actually want. Later, in Chapter 5, you'll have a chance to dig deeper with the full Autopilot Audit — a practical checklist that shows common ways autopilot shows up across each of the five SPiCE pillars.

Once you can spot the gap between the two, you stop being quite so easily steered by whatever narrative is currently in front of you. That same discipline of choosing your frame shows up in a simple daily practice I started using after my own time away.

The AM Reframe – A Simple Daily Practice

One personal exercise I've adopted since my sabbatical is what my weekly men's group calls the AM Reframe. Our pastor Rich shared it one Sunday as the best way to set yourself up not only for a good day but for a truly healthy one amid all the noise and madness we get assaulted with the second we wake up. It's really simple: be disciplined about what media and messaging you consume first thing in the morning. Because what you consume will consume you if you're not careful.

If you start the day with social media, you're booting up with a frame of envy and comparison — everyone else's highlight reel makes your own life feel smaller. If you start your day with the news, your day is framed with anxiety and a low-grade sense that the world is spinning out of control. If you start your day with work emails, you set the tone for stress and a reactive mindset before you've even had coffee. But if you start with meditation or prayer, you set a calm, centered frame that keeps the algorithm from grabbing the wheel.

Cognitive Sovereignty

The AM Reframe is a simple daily practice, but it points to something deeper: the personal right and practice of independently evaluating the stories, assumptions, and information that come at you, rather than automatically accepting what the algorithm, media, or others feed you. This is Cognitive Sovereignty.

It gives you clear, independent thinking and mental freedom. You stop living in someone else's narrative and begin writing your own.

Yet Cognitive Sovereignty is constantly under threat from four quiet thieves:

1. The endless (and often mendacious) algorithm feed designed to keep you engaged, outraged, or reassured.

2. Cultural and social pressure to adopt popular opinions without examination.

3. Old mental habits and confirmation bias that feel comfortable but keep you small.

4. Echo chambers and tribal thinking that reinforce existing beliefs while shielding us from any perspective that might challenge them.

Cognitive Sovereignty Exercises

These prompts, built around the quiet thieves above, help you examine the stories, assumptions, and information you've been living inside. Pick one or two that feel alive right now, grab your journal, and explore on your own terms.

Quiet Thief 1 – The endless (and often mendacious) algorithm feed

- **The Algorithm Audit** – Look at your main social media or news feeds. What emotions do they most often provoke — outrage, fear, reassurance, or comparison? How does that emotional pull shape what you believe?

- **The Engagement Trap** – When was the last time you kept scrolling because something made you angry or anxious? What would it look like to step away from the algorithm and think for yourself?

- **Curating Your Input** – If you could design your own information diet free from algorithmic manipulation, what sources or practices would you choose instead?

- **The Outrage Test** – Pick one story that recently triggered a strong emotional reaction in your feed. Ask yourself: "Is this information complete, or am I being emotionally steered?" Write what you discover.

Quiet Thief 2 – Cultural and social pressure to adopt popular opinions without examination

- **The Popular Opinion Check** – What belief or viewpoint do you hold mainly because it's widely accepted in your social circle? How would you feel if you questioned it?

- **The Fear of Disagreeing** – Where do you stay silent or go along with the group even when something doesn't feel right to you? What small step could you take toward intellectual honesty?

- **The Social Pressure Mirror** – Think of a recent conversation where you felt pressure to agree. What would it have looked like to speak your own truth instead?

- **Independent Thinking Practice** – Choose one current cultural or political topic. Research it and write down your honest view — not what you think you "should" believe, but what you actually think after careful consideration.

Quiet Thief 3 – Old mental habits and confirmation bias that feel comfortable but keep you small

- **The Confirmation Bias Check** – When was the last time you only sought out information that confirmed what you already believed? How did that limit your thinking?

- **The Comfortable Story** – What old mental habit or assumption about yourself or the world feels safe but may be holding you back? Write it down, then write the opposite view.

- **Intellectual Humility** – Think of a belief you've held for years. What evidence would it take for you to reconsider it? Are you truly open to that evidence?

- **The Growth Question** – What is one assumption you've been carrying that might no longer serve you? What would change if you released it and thought freshly about the topic?

Quiet Thief 4 – Echo chambers and tribal thinking

- **The Tribal Mirror** – Where do you notice yourself automatically aligning with your group's view without independently examining the evidence? What might open up if you stepped outside that circle for a moment?

- **Seeking the Other Side** – Pick a topic you feel strongly about. Deliberately seek out a thoughtful, well-reasoned argument from the opposing perspective. What shifts (if any) occur in your thinking?

- **Breaking the Bubble** – What sources, people, or communities do you tend to avoid because they challenge your current beliefs? What could happen if you engaged with them honestly?

- **Loyalty vs Truth** – Is there an area in your life where group loyalty feels more important to you than pursuing truth? What would intellectual honesty look like in that area?

Try some now, save some for later

You can start exploring these prompts right now if the spirit moves you — they're powerful even in small doses. But don't be surprised if they really come alive once you're actually on sabbatical, with the dedicated time and space to go deep without the usual noise of daily life pulling you away.

These prompts are just starting points. Adapt them, follow your curiosity, and remember: a sabbatical is your chance to stop living in someone else's story and start writing your own.

Once you've taken that first real step toward Cognitive Sovereignty — renewed confidence and the ability to think for yourself instead of letting the world think for you — you'll notice something bigger beginning to take shape.

Cognitive Sovereignty is only one leg of a larger framework I call the *Sovereignty Triangle*. This Triangle is the bigger idea behind SPiCE. It turns the five pillars from a simple dashboard into a complete system of personal ownership. It is built on three equal legs: *Cognitive Sovereignty, Body Sovereignty, and Spirit Sovereignty.*

Together, the Sovereignty Triangle is the deliberate act of taking back full ownership of your mind (choosing where you invest your mental energy instead of letting a career or algorithms run the show), your body (stepping off the hamster wheel of quick fixes, pills, and the pressure to outsource your health to anything outside yourself), and your spirit (finding the confidence to embrace your true purpose and faith even in a judgmental world) instead of quietly outsourcing them to stress, distraction, or default habits.

You'll find the complete definitions and benefits for each leg in the Glossary. For a deeper dive with practical journal exercises designed to strengthen all three prongs, turn to the Sovereignty Triangle section in the Appendix (or the companion workbook).

For now, simply notice how the work you just did on Cognitive Sovereignty already feels different when you imagine it working in harmony with your body and spirit. That harmony is where real, lasting change begins.

Once you've started reclaiming your own narrative, you're ready to point that story in a direction that actually fits the life you want — the purposeful direction you'll define in the very next chapter.

Chapter Three

Purpose: Aim High from Solid Ground

"By failing to prepare, you are preparing to fail."
—— Benjamin Franklin

Like any serious endeavor, your sabbatical needs a solid strategic foundation and clear direction. It's not a 'wing it' kind of thing—especially when the time and energy you're investing may be once-in-a-lifetime. Diving in cold and figuring it out as you go is a recipe for wasted days and unnecessary stress. Not everything has to be locked in granite, but the more strategic clarity you bring upfront, the higher the return. Sabbatical is designed to reduce anxiety, not add to it. Approach it accordingly.

Now that you've started reclaiming your own narrative in Chapter 2, it's time to point that story in a direction that actually fits the life you want.

Sabbatical Sandboxes - Where do you want to play?

Your first strategic move is to identify and name the high-level purpose(s) that will drive your sabbatical. This will set your trajectory and help you confidently prioritize what you need and what you want out of it. Most sabbaticals fall into one (or a blend) of four strategic ERGO Sandboxes: Exploration, Restoration, Growth, and Objective. Each is a rich, multi-dimensional playground. Some of you may already be carrying a clear Objective into this process—maybe it's been simmering for years, like travel, writing a book, or tackling a big life transition. Others are arriving more open-ended, ready to explore what emerges. Both are valid starting points; regardless, your ERGO purpose provides both a compass to guide and a foundation on which to build your strategy.

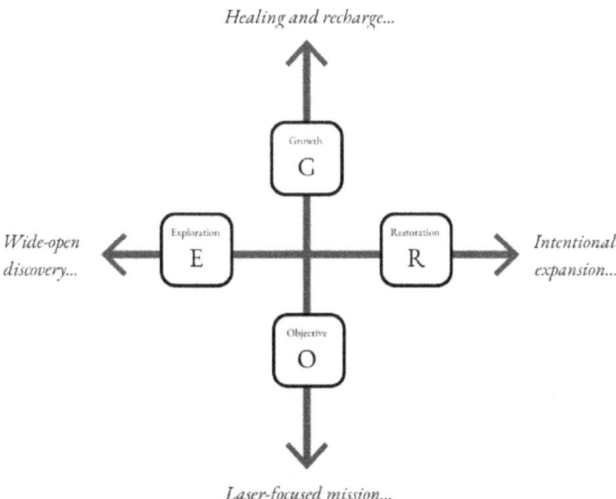

Sabbaticaleer's 4 ERGO Sandbox Directions

Exploration

Wide-open discovery. New roads, new curiosities, no rigid agenda. It's about gathering experiences that stretch your horizons and remind you life is bigger than the daily grind.

Restoration

Healing and recharge. Burnout, grief, caregiver fatigue, or years of high-output pressure have drained your reserves. This sandbox prioritizes deep rest, physical recovery, and emotional processing—so you can get back to baseline and stand tall again.

Real-life nod: My own sabbatical began here, after years of caregiving for my wife's chronic illness, parenting through the storm, career grind, and then losing both parents in a freak carbon monoxide accident. Restoration wasn't optional; it was the only way to refill the tank enough to even think about what came next.

Growth

Deliberate expansion. Building new skills, deepening knowledge, strengthening body and spirit, recalibrating priorities. Proactive: you emerge sharper, stronger, wiser for the long haul.

Real-life nod: While my sabbatical started grounded in Restoration, by the end, a pursuit of personal Growth emerged: leverage 27 years of agency branding expertise, personal loss, caregiving scars, and hard-won resets to become a Renewal

Specialist—redefining my second act by paying it forward. Turn those lessons into this book to help others spot their sabbatical cues, apply the SPiCE filter, and craft plans that truly reset their trajectory.

Objective

Targeted achievement with something specific already burning a hole in your pocket? You show up with a clear mission: write the book, complete that cross-country trek, launch the side venture, master a craft, build a legacy project, or finally finish what life kept interrupting. This sandbox carves out protected space to deliver on that one (or a few) big thing(s) you've carried too long.

Embrace the Blend

There's bound to be overlap here, and that's the beauty of it — sabbaticals aren't meant to be rigid silos. For instance, that Objective project you may have in mind will likely weave in elements of Exploration (uncovering fresh insights along the way), Growth (honing skills to pull it off), or Restoration (pausing to recharge when the push gets heavy). Depending on your headspace at any given time, you might shift gears: what feels like high-focus Growth work one week could turn fundamentally restorative the next, or open doors to Exploration you hadn't anticipated. ERGO isn't about picking one lane; it's about setting a course but also flexing as your needs evolve, letting the sandboxes feed each other for a more balanced ride.

Before we dive deeper, let's take a quick temperature check – what's pulling strongest right now of the four ERGO directions? Do one or two sandboxes resonate? No overthinking — this is just a gut scan of current headspace and energy, a quick self-assessment to notice what rises to the surface vs. falls away. Jot quick notes if something sparks.

Diving Deeper: Your *À La Carte* ERGO Menu

Sabbaticaleer has developed a multi-layered ERGO *a la carte* menu. Its a brainstorming tool to help you shift your mind-set to identify and dimensionalize your own custom sabbatical purpose. Flip ahead, if you like, and take a quick look at the full menu at the end of the chapter to see where we're headed. For now we will discuss and explore in layers.

Your job in this chapter is to take note of sandbox areas you might want to play in.

These are not must-dos —they're possibilities, ingredients you can pick from, combine, or set aside for what will become your custom recipe. These lists are also not meant to be exhaustive or complete—instead, they're really just thought starters. Think of them as a buffet: grab what looks good right now, taste a few combinations, leave the rest for later (or never). The goal here is to let ideas surface naturally so your sabbatical purpose starts to take shape around what actually matters to you.

Think of your *Purpose* as the big picture "why" – the high level sandbox (or blend of sandboxes) that feels most alive for you right now. *Dimensions* are the practical layers beneath it – the specific ways that Purpose actually shows up in daily life.

These are your a la carte menu of elements, goals, and priorities you can pick from, combine or set aside.

Grab your pencil or highlighter again. As we walk through each sandbox, circle or star any words or ideas that feel alive, intriguing, or even a little uncomfortable (those often point to the real gold). Jot a quick note next to them—why does it spark? What memory or feeling comes up? No right answers, just honest observation. And don't feel like you have to limit yourself. There will be plenty of time to review, reflect and prioritize later.

Exploration (E)

Exploration is about wide-open discovery, no rigid agendas. Core purposes to consider (and for you to further personally define) could include:

- Self-awareness
- Openness to the unknown
- Experimentation
- Growth and learning
- Meaning and purpose

Circle any that intrigue you. If you're drawn to Exploration, you might be craving space to wander without needing a destination yet—testing new paths, asking big questions, rediscovering curiosity that got buried under the grind. If you have a different way to articulate Exploration, that's even better! Write that down and circle it.

Restoration (R)

Restoration is about healing and recharge when reserves are low. Core purpose to ponder:

- Repair
- Revitalization
- Wholeness
- Resilience

Circle any concepts that resonate. And remember, you get to define what these words mean to you in your personal context. Restoration often shows up when burnout, grief, or long-term pressure has left you running on fumes. These purposes are about mending quietly but actively—giving yourself permission to refill the tank first.

Growth (G)

Growth is about a deliberate expansion into a new and improved version of yourself. Purpose areas to consider:

- Expansion
- Development
- Potential
- Authenticity
- Fulfillment

Note what lights you up. Growth is proactive—leveling up emotionally, mentally, physically, professionally—when you're ready to stretch beyond survival into something fuller and more authentic.

Objective (O)

The Objective sandbox reflects something you're already bringing to the party. Targeted achievement on something specific that maybe you've carried too long. Purpose areas to weigh:

- Clarity of Mission
- Focused Execution
- Milestone Achievement
- Legacy Building
- Targeted Fulfillment

Circle what feels urgent or meaningful. The Objective sandbox is for the non-negotiable mission already burning a hole in your pocket—writing the book, completing the trek, launching the venture, finishing what life kept interrupting. It's about carving out protected space to deliver. It's in this arena that you own articulation will likely be even more helpful.

Take a breath. Look back over your circles and stars. Which sandbox (or blend) feels strongest? Which purposes keep pulling your eye? This is your first real sketch of purpose—raw, honest, yours. You may find that you are drawn to aspects of all four, and that's fine too, for now. The point is to identify the sandbox concepts that feel most relevant to you.

Next rank them now, 1-4, with 1 being your top pull. Identifying your top two will sharpen focus as we build—maybe a primary sandbox with a secondary for support. Jot that rank on the worksheet too.

Drilling Down: Dimensionalizing Priorities for Deeper Clarity

Once you've identified what sparks from the Purpose layer, we're going to flip to the worksheet at the end of the chapter to dig deeper into their various Dimensions. These are the practical layers—where you start turning "maybe this" into "how might this actually look?" Again, *à la carte*: pick what fits, adapt what's close, skip what doesn't. Under each sandbox, the priorities break the work into manageable pieces. Here is what you can expect.

For **Exploration**, the internal landscape (emotional, cognitive, spiritual) invites quiet inner work, while the external world and creative expression push you outward—social connections, cultural immersion, artistic or physical play. Circle priorities that feel exciting or necessary.

Restoration gets concrete: physical rest & nourishment, emotional processing, social & spiritual support, and gentle time & pace. Highlight what you know you need most right now.

Growth layers internal (emotional, mental & spiritual), external (social, physical & professional), process (learning, reflection & change), motivation (intrinsic/extrinsic balance), and sustainable pace.

Objective focuses more on internal alignment and discipline, external resources and impact, clear process steps, passion-driven motivation, and paced timelines with buffers. Note which priorities feel essential to protect your mission.

Don't force final answers yet—just keep circling, jotting, noticing patterns. What combinations emerge? What feels energizing vs. draining? This is the foundation: your ERGO mix (or dominant sandbox) will guide every subsequent step toward a your custom sabbatical.

How I Built My Own ERGO Purpose – A Real-Life Example

It didn't happen in one tidy afternoon. For weeks I carried a simple notebook and let the question sit with me: What do I actually need and want from this sabbatical? I thought about it while walking the dog, daydreaming in the car, praying about it in the quiet of early mornings, and jotting notes whenever something felt alive. Defining its true purpose was just one facet.

After a couple of weeks I sat down to make sense of my wanderings. *Sabbaticaleer* developed the ERGO worksheet as a brainstorming short cut. Compared to my original notes, I would have ended up circling about fifteen different phrases from the full menu — pretty evenly spread across Exploration, Restoration, and Growth. My sabbatical was built first and foremost around Restoration so I could heal, then gradually shifted toward a balanced Growth focus with complimentary Exploration elements woven in.

Under Exploration I circled self-awareness, openness to the unknown (which later opened the door to the cognitive sovereignty idea), nature exploration (which became our family trip out west), and intellectual exploration (which led to this book).

Under Restoration I circled repair, resilience, rest and relaxation, finding meaning and purpose, connecting with loved ones, engaging in community, and sustainable practices (which later tied directly into the systems I built which I will mention later).

Under Growth I circled authenticity (another thread that led to my pursuit of cognitive sovereignty), spiritual growth, physical growth, and self-reflection.

I didn't force them into neat boxes. I just let the ideas breathe. Then I looked back at my SPiCE scores from Chapter 1 and started grouping the circled items by which pillars they would feed. That's when the "cords" started to form — clear threads that tied the sandboxes to the specific shifts I knew I needed.

What surprised me was how simple and grounding the whole exercise felt once I stopped trying to make it perfect. I didn't need a finished master plan on day one. I just needed a handful of honest anchors I could build from.

Those ERGO anchors became the seeds for everything that followed. In Chapter 9, when you brainstorm your own SPiCE goals and sabbatical ideas, you'll use this same simple process: let the priorities you circled here point the way, then let the ideas flow. The foundation is already forming — you're just giving it room to grow.

Connecting ERGO to Your SPiCE Pillars

Here's where patterns emerge, and strategy takes root. While ERGO names the high-level purpose and dimensions, your

SPiCE pillars (Spiritual, Physical, Intellectual, Currencies, Emotional) from Chapter 1 are how it touches every part of you. The two frameworks feed each other.

For example: A purpose anchored in Restoration might lean heavily on Physical rest, Emotional processing, and Spiritual wholeness—rebuilding reserves across multiple pillars. A pre-determined Objective you bring might demand an Intellectual SPiCE focus (new skills and discipline for the project), Currency investment (networks, resources), or Emotional resilience (pushing through doubt). Exploration often lights up Intellectual curiosity and Spiritual meaning, while weaving in Physical adventure or Emotional openness.

As we wrap up this chapter, take a moment to review your Chapter 1 SPiCE self-assessment. Which pillars feel depleted? Which are already strong? Now glance back at what you highlighted across your ERGO worksheet—which purposes naturally address those weak and strong spots?

By the end of this process, you're aiming to distill down to two per pillar. For now, don't limit yourself because there will surely be iterations to come.

Ultimately, sabbatical success boils down to two clear measures: (1) measurable positive shifts in your SPiCE scores—from pre-sabbatical baselines, through the journey, to post—and (2) your own custom big, medium, and small initiatives that will support your defined ERGO purpose, drive those SPiCE shifts, and tee you up for sustained health and well-being in life's second act.

A clear ERGO Purpose points you in the direction your future sabbatical and it various parts will follow. Looking around the corner, we will brainstorm corresponding goals (as well as ideas) that ensure your sabbatical makes the impact you want.

Your Homework

Look over the ERGO Worksheet on the next page to help you hone in. Rank the sandboxes 1-4 at the top, then highlight, circle, or check each Purpose and Dimension that sparks interest for you. Count the number of ideas you marked in each column and note it at the bottom—it's a simple way to see where your energy clusters. Feel free to add your own ideas or definitions too; this is your menu, and it is meant to be a jumping-off point, not necessarily comprehensive.

Next, identify and collect all the words/ideas that potentially address your sabbatical needs for each of your five SPiCE pillars. As days pass and you have time to reflect, try to distill your ERGO anchors down to size.

From there, create your own ERGO worksheet in your journal and begin identifying the words/ideas that best ladder up to your SPiCE needs.

Remember, to facilitate your journey, *Sabbaticaleer* offers free downloadable versions of this and other worksheets at sabbaticaleer.com.

ERGO *À La Carte* Menu

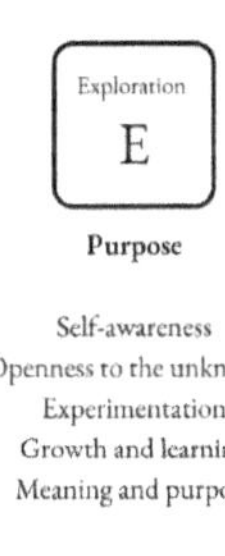

Purpose

Self-awareness
Openness to the unknown
Experimentation
Growth and learning
Meaning and purpose

Dimensions

Internal Landscape
Emotional exploration
Cognitive exploration
Spiritual exploration

External World
Social exploration
Cultural exploration
Nature exploration

Creative Expression
Artistic exploration
Physical exploration
Intellectual exploration

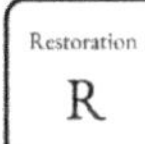

Purpose

Repair
Revitalization
Wholeness
Resilience

Dimensions

Physical
Rest & relaxation
Nourishment
Self-care practices

Mental and Emotional
Stress management
Processing difficult emotions
Finding meaning & purpose

Social and Spiritual
Connecting with loved ones
Engaging in community
Seeking professional help

Time and Pace
Personalization
Compassion and patience
Sustainable practices

Purpose

Expansion
Development
Potential
Authenticity
Fulfillment

Dimensions

Internal Focus
Emotional growth
Mental growth
Spiritual growth

External Focus
Social growth
Physical growth
Professional growth

Process
Continuous learning
Self-reflection
Openness to change

Motivation
Intrinsic motivation
Extrinsic motivation
Balancing both motivations

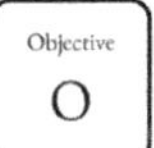

Purpose

Clarity of Mission
Focused Execution
Milestone Achievement
Legacy Building
Targeted Fulfillment

Dimensions

Internal Focus
Value-mission alignment
Discipline & resilience
Intrinsic progress satisfaction

External Focus
Gather resources & networks
Create community impact
Seek validation & recognition

Process
Break into steps
Track & adjust progress
Integrate feedback loops

Motivation
Passion-driven mission
Balance urgency & sustainability
Celebrate small wins

Time and Pace
Realistic timelines & buffers
Integrate other sandboxes
Pace to prevent burnout

Chapter Four

Image vs Identity

"The happiness of those who want to be popular depends on others; the happiness of those who seek pleasure fluctuates with moods outside their control; but the happiness of the wise grows out of their own free acts."

— Marcus Aurelius

Once you've named a clear ERGO Purpose in Chapter 3 and started reclaiming your own narrative in Chapter 2, something else quietly shifts. You realize the next question isn't just "What do I believe?" but "How do I show up?" That's where image and identity start their own quiet dance.

Image is the version of you the world sees — the persona you've worn for years because it was safe, expected, rewarded, perhaps even curated. Identity is the deeper truth underneath: who you actually are when the spotlight is off and the performance ends. Earlier, we stepped out of the cave and started reclaiming authorship of our own thoughts. Now we step fully into the sunlight and face a different challenge: making sure the story we tell the world matches the one we're finally telling ourselves.

When I cashed out after twenty-seven years in advertising, I was grateful to leave at the same time as Ben, the agency's founder. For seventeen of those years, I had worked at the independent shop that once bore his name. Our exit realities were different but overlapping: I was a partner walking away from the agency, while Ben was selling the company he had built. Regardless, we both walked the same emotional tightrope — moving from the known to the unknown. The question we kept circling back to was simple yet loaded:

How much of our image was tied to our agency and career, and how would our identity shift once we left?

I realized this transition would be the first real test of whether I could apply the same honesty to my own life — the underlying practice I was already developing and would eventually define, through my sabbatical and beyond, as cognitive sovereignty.

Image and Identity are two sides of the same coin, and they were the bread and butter of my advertising career. From a branding perspective, both try to capture the essence of something — a company, a product, or even a person. Image is the surface: the logo, the slogan, the carefully curated social feed. It's what others see — the billboard you can swap out based on market conditions. Identity is the beating heart beneath: the mission, the guiding principles, the unique story that can't be faked. Image is a projection. Identity is soul.

The critical difference lies in control and intentionality. Brands (and people) actively sculpt their image, manipulating perceptions to reach specific audiences. Identity, however, is shaped by experiences, beliefs, and values. It evolves more slowly and is far less controllable. When you first meet, date, or hire someone, you're interacting with their image. It takes time — and often stress — to see the identity underneath.

In the language we explored in a previous chapter, image is largely perception — the curated version shaped by what you think others want to see — while identity is perspective — the deeper truth you choose to stand in once you step back and audit the story.

Yet image and identity are not separate. A strong brand has an image that authentically reflects its identity, creating coherence and trust. The same is true for people. When your inner identity informs your outward image, you radiate genuine confidence and connection. Alignment sparks authenticity. Misalignment creates tension.

For me, the misalignment had been building for some time. Life circumstances finally forced my hand. The image I had worked so hard to project — the sharp tip of the spear assigned the best accounts and new-business pitches — was no longer sustainable. I was exhausted and ready to shed it. Ben's situation was more complex. He had recently remarried and was cashing out for a new life he had earned. On the surface it looked like the perfect exit, but the agency was rebranding itself away from him and his legacy. His name was no longer on the door. The narrative had shifted to a turnaround story. Ben got a fair price, but I could tell he was mortgaging part of his identity to get it.

Atlanta-based *Sabbaticaleer* loves Baseball Hall of Famer Greg Maddux. When asked how he stayed so low-key and humble through 355 wins and four Cy Young Awards, Maddux replied, "You think about the things that are important to you, and I guess it's never really been high on the list, worrying about what other people think." Maddux is a living example of someone whose identity spoke louder than any projected image.

Actions speak louder than words. Your actions are the truest expression of your identity — what you actually do when the spotlight is off. Your words, on the other hand, are often part of the image you project to the world — carefully chosen to shape how others see you.

In our contemporary world, nowhere is the image-identity tension on display more than on social media. It gives us a platform to connect and craft carefully curated versions of ourselves, yet it also intensifies the pressure to perform. Many of us chase an idealized online persona that drifts further and further from who we really are. The dopamine hit of likes becomes addictive, and suddenly we're living for the feed instead of for ourselves.

But social media is just one stage where this drama plays out — especially for those who have already stepped away from it or never engaged much in the first place. The same tension shows up in parent groups at school, neighborhood expectations, club memberships, workplace culture, and even hobby circles where we quietly perform the "right" version of ourselves to fit in. Sabbatical gives you the rare chance to step back from all these stages and ask the deeper question:

Am I living for the image I'm projecting, or for the identity I actually want to carry into my second act?

Every day life creates a natural tension between our personal sense of identity and image. Image plays a critical role in relationships and business, but emotional well-being is based on alignment, not conflict, between the two. Have you been aiming high with an identity grounded in power, or aiming low with an image grounded in force? Is it time for a realignment?

The tension between image and identity has always been part of the human condition. Let's look at a few stories — secular and sacred — to see it in action.

F. Scott Fitzgerald's The Great Gatsby (1925)

Jay Gatsby projects an opulent image of effortless success — mansion, parties, dazzling persona — all designed to win back Daisy Buchanan. Beneath the glitter is a man haunted by his past and driven by an idealized memory. The clash between the billboard he built and the melancholic identity he hid ultimately leads to his downfall. Gatsby's story is a poignant reminder of the dangers of chasing an external image at the expense of your authentic self.

Mary Shelley's Frankenstein (1818)

Victor Frankenstein projects the image of a brilliant scientist conquering nature. His true identity, however, is riddled with guilt, self-loathing, and anxiety over the ethical consequences of his creation. The agonizing gap between his projected brilliance and his tormented inner self drives the novel's chilling progression — a cautionary tale about unchecked ambition and the cost of ignoring your deeper self.

The Conversion of Saul (Acts 9)

Saul strode the world stage with an image of unwavering piety and righteous persecution of Christians. On the road to Damascus, a blinding light shattered that facade. The man who emerged was Paul — zealous spirit transmuted into a burning passion for the very message he once condemned. His Damascus moment was a seismic shift: image and identity finally aligned in a powerful symphony of grace.

The Parable of the Prodigal Son (Luke 15:11-32)

The younger son begins with youthful bravado, projecting an image of independence and freedom as he demands his inheritance and squanders it. Stripped bare in the pigsty, his image crumbles. In that moment of hunger and hollowness, he remembers his father's love. His return home is the shedding of the mask — a raw plea for reconnection with his true self. The embrace isn't just a reunion; it's the fusion of image and identity.

Check out Appendix III to see *Sabbaticaleer's* selected reading recommendations that can help you dig deeper across the different SPiCE Pillars.

A Mind Wide Open

One of the best things I did during my sabbatical was to go in with an open mind and be present with the people I encountered from all walks of life. If we suddenly played in the sandbox of sabbatical or personal growth, I tried to track down and read any recommended books or resources. I ended up with a big stack and read most of them.

My friend Doug recommended one book in particular while we were on a mission trip building homes in Ecuador: David R. Hawkins' *Power vs. Force*. It's a challenging but ultimately satisfying read. Hawkins, an M.D. and Ph.D. and an acknowledged authority in consciousness research, explores the dynamics of human consciousness and how emotions and beliefs shape our lives.

He argues that Identity is a concept of Power while Image is a concept of Force.

Power is effortless influence through truth, love, and integrity. It emanates from a high level of consciousness and attracts positive outcomes. Force is manipulation through coercion, fear, and control. It stems from lower levels of consciousness and ultimately weakens itself and others.

A simple example is Mahatma Gandhi. Instead of meeting British force with force, he harnessed the power of moral authority and nonviolent resistance — *Satyagraha*, or "truth-force." His commitment to truth and justice prevailed over colonial oppression and continues to inspire movements for justice worldwide.

Hawkins' framework offers a valuable lens for anyone on a sabbatical journey. Higher levels of consciousness (love, compassion, understanding) support a deeper connection with your authentic identity. Lower levels (pride, vanity, fear) push us toward projecting an image that may not align with who we truly are. By recognizing and challenging the ego's role in crafting a false self, we can move toward a more harmonious integration of image and identity — and liberate ourselves from the slavery of meeting others' expectations. In short:

Power is what cognitive sovereignty looks like when it's lived out loud.

With those ideas fresh in mind, here are ten journal prompts designed to help you peel back the layers and get honest about the masks you wear. They're especially powerful when you have the dedicated time and space of your sabbatical to deep-dive into them. That said, there's no time like the present — pick as many as feel useful right now, grab your journal, find a quiet moment, and explore on your own terms.

Journal Prompts to help Unmask Your Image vs. Identity

These are thought-starters to help you peel back the layers and get honest about the masks you wear. Pick as many as you like, grab your journal, and explore on your own terms.

Mirror, Mirror on the Wall Describe your "public persona" — the image you project to the world. What words capture how you want others to see you? How consistent is this with your inner sense of self?

Beyond the Persona As you peel back the layers, consider the energy behind them. Which masks feel heavy and draining? Which ones feel lighter and more expansive? Can you identify unconscious patterns that keep you clinging to the heavier ones?

Roots of the Facade Where do you think your desire for a specific image came from? Family expectations, societal pressures, or personal aspirations? Can you identify any turning points that shaped your self-presentation?

Voices in the Void Listen to the inner voices that whisper about your true self. What desires, fears, and dreams do they reveal? Are there recurring themes or conflicts?

The Escape from the Cave Have you ever experienced moments when the shadows on Plato's cave wall started to lose their hold? What triggered those glimpses of your true self, and how did they change your perception of your image and identity?

Beyond the Likes Imagine living in a world without social media or external validation. How would your self-perception and priorities change? What would matter most to you?

Dare to Be Unfamiliar Can you identify any aspects of your true self that feel hidden or silenced? What would it take to bring them into the light, even if they don't align with your current image?

Rewriting the Narrative If you could craft a new story for yourself that authentically reflects your inner world, what would it be? What values and passions would guide your journey?

Authentic Connections Who feels like a safe space where you can shed the masks and be your true self? How do these relationships nourish your sense of identity?

Beyond the Sabbatical How do you imagine your relationship with image and identity will evolve as your sabbatical journey unfolds? What steps will you take to live more authentically?

Once you've spent time with these prompts, you'll likely have a clearer sense of the gap between the image you show the world and the identity you truly carry. That clarity is invaluable — because the next step in your sabbatical journey is learning how to measure and track the shifts you want to create. In the following chapter, we turn that inner work into a living dashboard so you can see real progress rather than just hope for it.

Chapter Five

Self-Reflection and Metrics Planning

"Your vision will become clear only when you can look into your own heart. Who looks outside, dreams; who looks inside, awakes."
— Carl Jung

We've arrived at a critical point in your sabbatical journey and we haven't even begun the fun part of thinking of all the cool things you might do. But, don't worry, that's only few chapters away! Right now though you have one of the most important things to do first. Its time to do some personal heavy lifting and set up the systems that will track your sabbatical progress and formalize your pre-sabbatical benchmarks.

We've already tipped our hat to Socrates: knowing yourself is the root of wisdom. But knowing without tracking is like sailing without a compass. You're the CEO of this sabbatical — not a tourist snapping selfies. Real progress shows up when you measure it: the shift from burnout to balance, the wins in healing and growth, keeping a living record of a once in a lifetime experience, the tangible steps toward the second act you want. This chapter gives you three simple, repeatable tools to build a living dashboard you can actually use:

Sabbatical Journal — your private vault (the foundation — set this up first)

SWOT Analysis— your strategic snapshot (do this early to see the landscape and inform your journey)

SPiCE Snapshots — your ongoing fuel gauge (regular check-ins to track movement)

Start with the journal. It's where everything gets captured. Get this right, and the rest flows.

Tool 1: Your Sabbatical Journal – Your Private Vault of Insight

As you dive into your sabbatical, your journal becomes the official log of transformation. It's a mirror for growth, a vault for ideas, proof of your grit, and a safeguard against losing the gold you're mining. Sabbaticals stir up depths—ignored emotions, fresh epiphanies, late-night million-dollar ideas, wisdom from chance conversations. Write them down, or they fade like a dream.

Why bother? Insight and inspiration are transitory unless you catch them. My journal swelled to nearly 300 pages over 321 days—packed with links, quotes, frustrations, breakthroughs, travel notes, progress updates, dreams, and the strategic backbone of my planning. Rediscovering a long-forgotten entry months (or years) later remains one of the most satisfying returns on the investment. It helped me weave yoga's calm into daily life and integrate hard-won purpose post-sabbatical.

For another example, picture Sarah, a mid-career teacher on a six-month break after burnout: her entries tracked the slow shift from "overwhelmed by grading" to "excited about mentoring kids," ultimately sparking a pivot to coaching. That's the power of a consistent record.

Don't worry if you've never considered yourself a "good writer." This isn't literature; it's a private record. No one ever needs to see it but you. A good portion of mine was simply a collection of article links, personal observations, quotes, metrics, and raw thoughts. Just let it flow. You'll surprise yourself—and you'll thank yourself later.

Your journal can be equal parts travel log, progress report, idea bank, thoughts organizer, metrics tracker, and cherished memento. How much you invest in it directly determines how much you carry forward. The more consistently you capture, the more you'll rediscover significant, unique insights when you need them most.

Go Digital (with Room for Your Rhythm)

Sabbaticaleer strongly recommends a digital, cloud-based journal as the core system. Even if you love the romance of a leather-bound notebook, don't shortchange yourself by relying only on longhand. Digital gives you instant access, searchability, automatic backups, and the ability to add photos, links, or voice notes on the go.

I used a password-protected WordPress.com blog (about $100/year to avoid ads; free options like Blogger work too). I tagged minimally at first (the five SPiCE pillars + "Metrics"), then grew to about 40 custom tags for recurring topics or categories from "Books read/to read" to "Fatherhood" to "Legacy" to my regular SPiCE score check-ins, and many more.

Whatever the entry, the goal was to tag it some way, somehow to allow easy access to patterns or trends or interest.

It turned my journal into a personal search engine — priceless when reconnecting with ideas or planning next steps. It remained active for years after my planned time off.

That said, many people find their own rhythm with analog — and that's perfectly fine. I actually used both: a handsome leather-bound journal for meditative flow and a digital version as the primary keeper. Hybrid works beautifully for lots of folks. The key is consistency: get the thoughts out, tag or date them, and review regularly.

Quick Start for Traction

Give your journal immediate love and momentum by copying over:

- Your "Best Self" reflection (the exercise below) plus any early SPiCE pillar insights.
- Your Day 1 SPiCE Self-Assessment from Chapter 1.
- Your ERGO progress from Chapter 3.
- A simple, honest entry on why you're taking (or needing) this sabbatical.

From there, aim to write something daily — even a short note, a quote, or a quick voice dictation. We'll talk about the simple power of this in Chapter 8: Systems that Stick. The upfront attention pays dividends. Your journal will become one of the most valuable assets of your sabbatical. You're mining for gold. Your journal is the vault. Protect it, use it, and watch how the riches compound.

Tool 2: SWOT Analysis – Your Strategic Snapshot

The SWOT — Strengths, Weaknesses, Opportunities, Threats — is your strategic snapshot, a classic business tool tailored here for personal sabbatical prep. Its objective is simple: give you a clear-eyed look at where you stand right now, so you can leverage what's working, shore up what's not, chase what's possible, and neutralize what could derail you.

Here's how each quadrant applies to your sabbatical journey:

Strengths: These are your internal superpowers — the positive qualities, skills, or resources you control that can fuel your renewal.

Weaknesses: These are your internal hurdles — the areas you struggle with or negative aspects under your control that need shoring up.

Opportunities: These are external chances or factors you can seize to advance your sabbatical.

Threats: These are external challenges or risks that could hold you back.

Use the SWOT Worksheet template at the end of the chapter as a starting point — keep it raw, 10–15 minutes per quadrant. Revisit it in your journal to track how your sabbatical turns weaknesses into strengths and threats into triumphs. Consider asking trusted friends or family for their observations. No wrong answers; just truth as you see it today. This simple snapshot turns vague ideas into strategic clarity — one page at a time.

Tool 3: SPiCE Snapshots – Your Ongoing Dashboard

With your journal rolling and SWOT mapped (or at least underway), add the fuel gauge: SPiCE Snapshots. This is your repeatable, central measurement system — the one check-in you return to again and again to track traction, movement, and real success.

Rate each pillar 1–10 on a regular basis - and always before/after major initiatives. Jot down at least one honest sentence per pillar explaining the number — those details reveal patterns. Are your levels rising, holding steady, or slipping? Numbers and direction tell the story.

I eventually created a simple spreadsheet table in my journal where I could note the date and and add a new row of scores and watch them stack up over time. The numbers show the trend but written comments you capture for each pillar are the real gold over time.

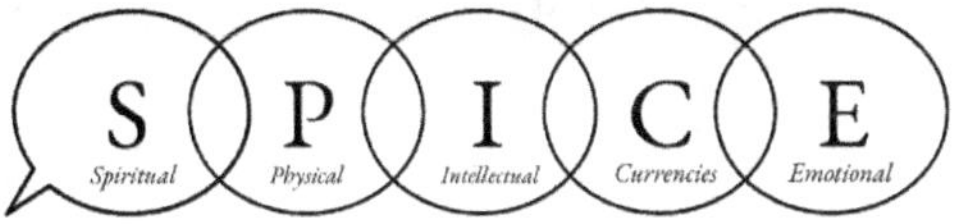

	S *Spiritual*	P *Physical*	I *Intellectual*	C *Currencies*	E *Emotional*
	10	10	10	10	10
Thriving	9	9	9	9	9
	8	8	8	8	8
	7	7	7	7	7
Surviving	6	6	6	6	6
	5	5	5	5	5
	4	4	4	4	4
	3	3	3	3	3
Dying	2	2	2	2	2
	1	1	1	1	1

<u>Scale</u>

8–10 = *Thriving* (healthy, strong) 4–7 = *Surviving* (marginal, holding but not thriving) 1–3 = *Dying* (critically low, screaming for attention)

My Arc – From Sabbatical Start to End

Day 1: sea of red and yellow warning lights—no green in sight. Burnout, grief, caregiver fatigue, ad-world grind—I was circling the drain. By Day 321, I was thriving with green lights dominating my dashboard. The journey wasn't linear; there were dips. But the Snapshot forced honesty and spotlighted what moved the needle including: yoga for Physical/Emotional, deep reflection for Spiritual, and family connections for Currencies.

My Day 1 vs Day 321 Scores

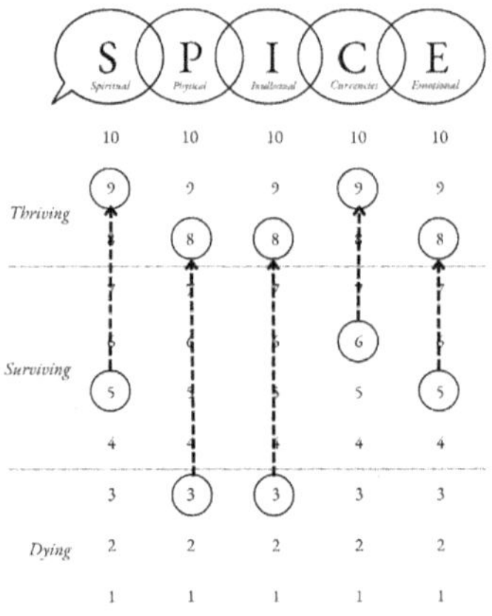

When I shifted out of sabbatical, I wasn't returning to easy street – life's pressures and realities were waiting for me with knives out. Physically, I was still at the front end of my reinvention, but comprehensively, I was prepared for my re-entry – recharged across all five SPiCE pillars and well equipped with new support systems and with a keen awareness that the work continued.

Best Self Reflection

Can you recall a time in your life when most or all of your SPiCE pillars were firing on all cylinders — when you felt like the very best version of yourself?

For me, that time was when I was 29. Recently married, living in a new city a thousand miles from home, still basically newlyweds. Before kids, before the grind took hold. Everything felt possible. Everything was still in front of us. To this day, Elizabeth and I celebrate our birthdays as the anniversaries of our 29th.

Now it's your turn. Think back to a season when you felt most alive, balanced, and true to yourself. Write about it in your journal. What was happening? How did your days feel? Why does that time still stand out to you?

If you can, estimate what your SPiCE scores might have been during that period. This "Best Self" memory will serve as a powerful, positive benchmark as you build your sabbatical plan and work toward getting back to — or even surpassing — that level of vitality.

Pitfalls to Watch

- Perfectionism — don't chase instant all-green; steady progress is the win.
- Avoidance — skipping when things feel rough (that's exactly when you need the mirror most).

- Over-analysis — these are data points, not verdicts. Keep notes concise and kind.

Three simple systems: your journal as a vault for capture, SWOT as a map for the landscape, SPiCE Snapshot as a fuel-tank dashboard for ongoing truth. Use them consistently, and your sabbatical shifts from guesswork to deliberate, measurable renewal. All roads lead back here.

There you have it. The foundations of your sabbatical metrics plan.

Homework – Chapter Questions / Prompts

1. Am I thinking Digital or analog journal, or both—and why?
2. Do a first draft of my SWOT.
3. What did my initial SWOT reveal?
4. Which quadrant surprised me most?
5. How do my strengths support my emerging ERGO purpose?
6. What one weakness or threat could derail my sabbatical?
7. What's my current SPiCE Snapshot and what's it telling me?
8. Which pillar is screaming for the most help right now?
9. How will I make these three tools (vault, map, dashboard) stick?
10. **Autopilot Audit** – Look back at your current SPiCE scores. As we discussed in Chapter 2, where might you still be running on autopilot? Turn to the next page and complete the Autopilot Audit. Circle or journal the patterns that feel familiar. Bring what you notice back into your journal and your next SPiCE Snapshot.

Autopilot Audit

(for use with your SPiCE self-assessment)

Most of us run parts of our lives on autopilot without realizing it. Autopilot almost always begins as perception — the fast, unexamined reaction that feels automatic and true. The lists below show common ways this shows up across each SPiCE pillar. Use them as a mirror while you score your current levels. Notice which ones land. Circle or journal the ones that feel familiar. You don't need to fix everything at once. Just see clearly where perception is still driving and where a deliberate shift in perspective might free you.

Spiritual

- Going through the motions of faith or purpose (or lack thereof) without ever asking if the story still fits.
- Running the same Sunday routine or morning ritual for years without checking whether it still feeds your actual sense of meaning.
- Assuming the purpose that got you this far is the same purpose that will carry you into the next act.
- Quietly outsourcing your inner life to whatever the culture (or your old self) says a "good" second act should look like.
- Feeling a low-grade spiritual restlessness but treating it as normal instead of a signal.

Physical

- Keeping the body driving on the same fuel and schedule even when the warning lights are flashing.
- Waking up stiff or tired and immediately reaching for the same coffee-and-push-through fix without checking what the body is actually asking for.
- Treating exercise (or the lack of it) as a fixed identity rather than a choice you can still update.
- Ignoring the slow accumulation of small physical warnings because "I've always been able to tough it out."
- Letting the calendar decide how much sleep and recovery you get instead of choosing it.

Intellectual

- Defending a comfortable set of opinions without testing them.
- Defending a long-held opinion the moment it gets challenged, before you've even examined the new information.
- Scrolling the same trusted sources and feeling confirmed rather than informed.

- Treating your current skill set or knowledge base as finished instead of open to expansion.
- Hearing a contrary view and instantly sorting it into "wrong" instead of "interesting — what if?"

Currencies

- Running the same money and relationship patterns because "that's just how it's always been."
- Spending or saving on the same autopilot patterns that made sense a decade ago without checking if they still serve the life you want now.
- Keeping relationship roles frozen in place ("I'm the one who always...") even when both people have changed.
- Measuring financial success by the same scoreboard you used in your thirties.
- Staying in a familiar relational dynamic because the alternative feels riskier than the mild dissatisfaction you already know.

Emotional

- Letting the old trigger fire the same response every time.

- Feeling the familiar flare of irritation, anxiety, or shutdown and immediately running the old response without pausing to name what's actually happening.

- Interpreting every setback through the same tired lens ("Here we go again") instead of asking what this particular moment is showing you.

- Letting yesterday's mood or last week's conflict set the emotional weather for today.

- Treating your emotional patterns as fixed personality rather than habits that can still be rewritten.

Circle what resonates. The goal is not perfection — it's simply to stop letting the old automatic version of the story run the whole show.

SWOT Worksheet - Your Strategic Snapshot

Strengths	*Weaknesses*
Opportunities	*Threats*

SPiCE Worksheet - Your Strategic Snapshot

Date: ________________

	S *Spiritual*	P *Physical*	I *Intellectual*	C *Currencies*	E *Emotional*
	10	10	10	10	10
Thriving	9	9	9	9	9
	8	8	8	8	8
	7	7	7	7	7
	6	6	6	6	6
Surviving	5	5	5	5	5
	4	4	4	4	4
	3	3	3	3	3
Dying	2	2	2	2	2
	1	1	1	1	1

Scale

8–10 = *Thriving* (healthy, strong)

4–7 = *Surviving* (marginal, holding but not thriving)

1–3 = *Dying* (critically low, screaming for attention)

Chapter Six

Ancient System, Modern Wisdom

"No man ever steps in the same river twice...it's not the same river, and it's not the same man."
—Heraclitus

You now have the tools to track your progress. But tracking is only part of the journey.

Some of the most powerful tools for real, lasting change come from ancient systems that have been helping people restore balance for thousands of years.

My yoga practice began as nothing more than a brainstormed strategy idea during my sabbatical planning. At the time, what I knew about yoga might have filled a short paragraph — certainly not a chapter's worth — but that paragraph would have noted its long, rich history as a practice of mind, body, and spirit. Given the sorry state of my pre-sabbatical SPiCE reserves, it checked enough boxes to be worth a shot.

In Chapter 4 we talked about the power of aligning your outward image with your deeper identity. A sabbatical gives you the rare freedom to explore fresh and unique ways to create real strength and balance across your five SPiCE pillars so that alignment actually sticks. But it also offers something deeper: the chance to reclaim full-spectrum sovereignty over your mind, your body, and your spirit.

This chapter takes you through why yoga became such a foundational practice for me and gives you a frame of reference as you move forward finding your own custom path. You don't have to embrace yoga specifically. What matters is discovering the systems and practices that strengthen all five of your SPiCE pillars in a way that feels authentic and sustainable for you.

The Nickel Tour

On Day 1 of my sabbatical my body felt like an achy foreign object — soft in the middle, weak, stiff, and out of balance. What stared back in the mirror didn't inspire confidence. I was fried, mentally and physically running on empty. Ten-plus years and countless hours later, yoga remains the single most powerful fulcrum I have found for real, lasting renewal.

Yoga as a Real-Time Dashboard

The first great thing about yoga is that it meets you exactly where you are — physically, mentally, and energetically — every time you step on the mat. Gravity becomes your dance partner. It's not simply something to fight against. In yoga, you learn to move both with it and against it — yielding where it serves you and resisting where it builds strength, stability, and surprising flexibility.

That real-time feedback is one of the reasons I came to love simple, functional tests like the "sit-to-stand." From a seated position on the floor, can you stand up without using your hands? It's a surprisingly revealing check of strength, balance, and mobility — and research shows that people who can do it easily tend to live longer. Yoga trains exactly those qualities.

The second great thing is that yoga functions as a whole-body self-awareness interface — a personal dashboard of your physical, mental, and energetic state in any given moment. Your breath, posture, and presence give you immediate data on where your SPiCE reserves actually sit that day. No app required.

"What's the Biggest Benefit of Having a Yoga Practice?"

I asked a motley crew of my yoga bros from the gym this one basic question. Their answers ranged from a single word to full paragraphs, and every one hit different parts of the SPiCE map. Their experience ran from less than two years to more than eleven.

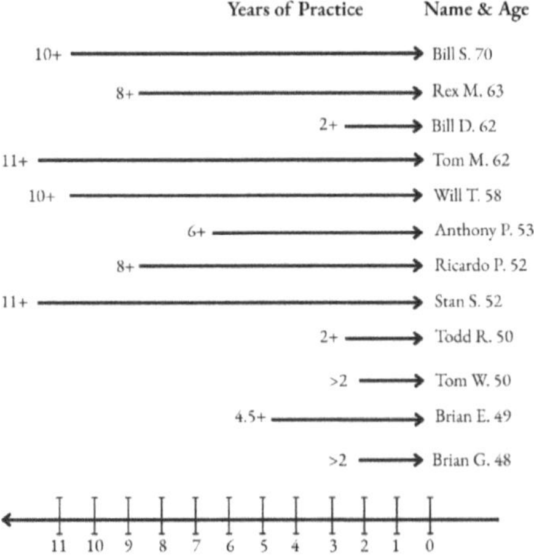

Here's what they said — no BS, just straight talk from the mat when asked: *"For You - Personally - What's the Biggest Benefit of Having a Yoga Practice?"*

Tom W. (50, practicing <2 years) kept his answer practical: "Stretching and strength training without the impact and strain that running, cycling, and weight lifting cause... it improves my flexibility as I age." Exactly right. The physical payoff alone is worth the price of admission.

Rex (63, 8+ years) gave the shortest, sharpest answer: "Equanimity." I love that word. It's the high-level mental and even spiritual benefit that sits on top of everything else. Equanimity's antonym is anxiety — yoga is a real-time, pharmaceutical-free anxiety neutralizer.

e·qua·nim·i·ty

/ˌekwəˈnimədē,ˌēkwəˈnimədē/

noun: equanimity

1. mental calmness, composure, and evenness of temper, especially in a difficult situation.: "he accepted both the good and the bad **with equanimity**".
2. antonyms: anxiety

"Seek Equanimity" would have been a perfect sabbatical SPiCE goal for me, and one I've since integrated thanks to Rex.

Brian E. (49, 4.5+ years) nailed the mental side: "Yoga has quieted my mind and taught me about my breath... breathing in balance with movement."

Anthony N. (53, 6+ years) described the flow: "As a person with a busy mind... those sixty to seventy-five minutes of flowing... disconnected from everyday living, but connected through breath and movement and a mind free of thought besides what I'm doing in the moment, is the greatest benefit."

Bill D. (62, 2+ years) went straight for the mental and emotional benefits: "The biggest benefit I receive in practicing yoga is mental strength and relaxation."

Ricardo P. (52, 8+ years) captured the deeper journey: "From my personal experience, yoga has been my guiding compass on a lifelong journey of self-awareness. It's the tool that's helped me break free from living on autopilot, enabling me to lead a more purposeful and meaningful life." Yes – awareness of and freedom from the all too easy autopilot mode of life.

Disengaging the auto-pilot function is a peak sabbatical experience.

Bill S. (70, 10+ years; a trumpet player and runner) tied it back to the breath and finding inner peace: "Breathing in balance with movement... when we are totally engaged in one activity is when we find our peace and happiness."

Stan S. (52, 11+ years) went deep: "The mental benefit is the sense of belonging to a community of like-minded individuals." He also added that yoga helps him "better accept the things in life that are outside of my control. So in essence, Yoga helps me to control stress." There's Stan channeling his *pharm-free equanimity*!

Brian G. (48, >2 years) keeps it real: "Without a doubt, the greatest benefit to yoga is mental. I came to yoga for the physical benefits, but I quickly realized that yoga gives me an hour a day where I can focus on nothing but my breath and my movements. My old way of dealing with stresses or offenses was with anger. Now, I can return to my breath at any time to center myself and 'return to my mat' no matter where I am."

Every guy brought something different, yet they all pointed to the same truth: yoga meets you where you are and gives back exactly what you need that day.

Sabbaticaleer's Sovereignty Triangle

Yoga is an excellent sabbatical practice because it's something you're inherently doing over time. In those first 321 days, I saw changes in my body I never thought possible — strength, balance, and flexibility showing up week after week like quiet proof that real renewal was happening. Because of my longtime interest in photography, I began to see my yoga mats as living time-lapse film — rolls of space-time emulsion where every mark, every smudge, became a tangible and meta record of my movement and breath.

The mat remembers what the mind forgets.

That visible, accumulating record became a powerful daily reminder that real change doesn't happen in one dramatic moment. It happens through consistent, repeated practice — one breath, one pose, one session at a time. The mat literally held the evidence of my own renewal.

Now, more than a decade later, I'm grateful to have found a system that delivers across all three dimensions of what I call the *Sovereignty Triangle — Sabbaticaleer's* simple but powerful framework made up of three equal legs: *Cognitive Sovereignty, Body Sovereignty, and Spirit Sovereignty.*

This Triangle is the bigger unifying philosophy behind SPiCE that turns the five pillars from a simple dashboard into a complete system of personal ownership.

Cognitive Sovereignty is the personal right and practice of independently evaluating the stories, assumptions, and information that come at you instead of automatically accepting what the algorithm, media, or others feed you. It gives you clear, independent thinking and mental freedom.

Body Sovereignty is the personal right and practice of honoring and caring for your body as the sacred vessel that carries your entire life, rather than outsourcing it to chronic stress, default habits, quick pharmaceutical fixes, or unrealistic external standards. It builds sustained physical energy, vitality, strength, and resilience.

Spirit Sovereignty is the personal right and practice of staying deeply connected to your own sense of purpose, values, awe, and something greater than yourself, rather than outsourcing meaning to external approval, cultural noise, or constant busyness. It creates a steady sense of inner peace and a centered, purposeful life.

Together, the Sovereignty Triangle is a deliberate act of taking back full ownership of your mind, body, and spirit from the Quiet Thieves — those small, everyday habits and thought patterns like endless scrolling, people-pleasing, comparison, overthinking, and living on autopilot — that quietly steal your Cognitive, Body, and Spirit sovereignty without you even noticing. The real benefit is lasting clarity of mind, sustained physical energy and resilience, and a steady inner peace that extends far beyond your sabbatical.

Yoga became my daily practice for living the Sovereignty Triangle out in real time — clearing mental noise, rebuilding physical strength and presence, and reconnecting me to something greater than myself.

Yoga Is a System and an Ever-Evolving Practice

I was first introduced to the power of systems versus goals by Scott Adams, the Dilbert creator and author. In his words, "A goal is a specific outcome you want; a system is a repeatable process that increases your chances of success over time." Goals can leave you feeling like a failure until you hit them, but systems give you daily wins, steady progress, and the specific attributes — consistency, adaptability, built-in feedback — that actually deliver the results you're after. Yoga is the perfect example of that kind of system — not a one-and-done target, but a repeatable practice that quietly compounds into real sovereignty:

It protects Cognitive (mind) Sovereignty by quieting the mental noise, Body Sovereignty by rebuilding strength and resilience from the inside out, and Spirit Sovereignty by creating space to align with something greater than yourself.

Yoga'a philosophical system aims to unite one's physical, mental, and spiritual facets into a harmonious whole. The Sanskrit word for yoga (*Yuj*) means "to yoke or unite." Its roots date back to the classical period, starting around the 5th century BC when Patanjali's *Yoga Sutras* introduced the framework with the *Eight Limbs of Yoga*. Still at work today, they serve as a path to holistic growth.

Yama – Ethical restraints and moral disciplines – *how we treat others*

Niyama – Personal observances and self-discipline – *how we treat ourselves*

Asana – Physical postures and body awareness

Pranayama – Breath control and regulation of life force

Pratyahara – Withdrawal of the senses and turning inward

Dharana – Concentration and one-pointed focus

Dhyana – Meditation and sustained awareness

Samadhi – Absorption, union, and a state of blissful oneness

Most modern classes in gyms and studios focus primarily on two of those limbs — physical posture and breath control. But depending on the teacher and the day, you might be exposed, at least conceptually, to any of the eight. One of the things that first attracted me to yoga was that every limb philosophically aims high, ethically and morally, and mirrors other systems I already lean on.

Yoga is also an ever-evolving *Practice*. The word "practice" itself implies ongoing development, personal exploration, and refinement rather than simple mastery. Yoga is about progress and presence, never perfection. For many of us it becomes a lifelong journey. As Heraclitus reminds us, we are constantly changing — and so is our yoga practice. Each session presents new opportunities to explore our limitations, refine our alignment, and deepen our understanding of ourselves.

Yoga Practice — Sabbaticaleer's Working Definition

Yoga has ancient roots stretching back thousands of years, originating on the Indian subcontinent. It takes many forms across the eight limbs. For the purposes of this book, *Sabbaticaleer* defines a yoga practice as a holistic discipline that combines physical postures (*asanas*), breathing exercises (*pranayama*), meditation, and ethical principles to support physical, mental, and spiritual well-being. It aims to build flexibility, strength, relaxation, and mindfulness while fostering a sense of inner peace and gratitude. Yoga can be adapted across many styles and levels of intensity, making it accessible to people of different ages and fitness levels.

This definition is admittedly imperfect, but *Sabbaticaleer* likes it because it offers a useful comparative checklist when evaluating other practices or activities. How well does something stack up across all five SPiCE pillars? The practices that meaningfully touch multiple pillars at once are often the ones worth prioritizing in your sabbatical plan.

The Breath, The Whole Body, and Gratitude

A. The Power of the Breath

From the very first yoga class or study session, one thing stands out above everything else: the breath. In Sanskrit it's called *Prana* — life force or vital energy. We breathe automatically every day without thinking about it, but yoga turns that unconscious act into a conscious bridge between body, mind, and spirit.

Several of the guys I interviewed — Brian E., Tony N., and Brian G. among them — zeroed in on the same thing when I asked about their biggest benefit: the breath quiets the busy mind, teaches balance with movement, and gives them a reliable way to center themselves anywhere, anytime. It's the anchor that turns yoga from exercise into something deeper.

While *yin* and *yang* come from Chinese Taoism rather than traditional Indian yoga, the symbol captures well what's happening on the mat. Inhale is the bright, expansive *yang* energy that fills you with fresh oxygen and opens the body. Exhale is the calm, inward *yin* that releases tension and grounds you. Each full breath — inhale and exhale in perfect rhythm — creates a holistic flow that nourishes both body and mind.

Like Heraclitus' ever-changing river, the poses constantly shift and change, mirroring the ever-moving current of life. Your breath becomes the steady guide that tells the body when to expand, open, reach up on the inhale, and when to release, ground, and fold on the exhale. Holding a pose isn't about freezing in a perfect shape; it's about finding balance and adapting inside the movement.

This is how yoga prepares you for life's constant changes.

B. A Whole Body Practice

If the first great thing about yoga is that it meets you wherever you are, the second great thing is that it's a whole-body experience. It's like having access to a real-time dashboard for your entire being.

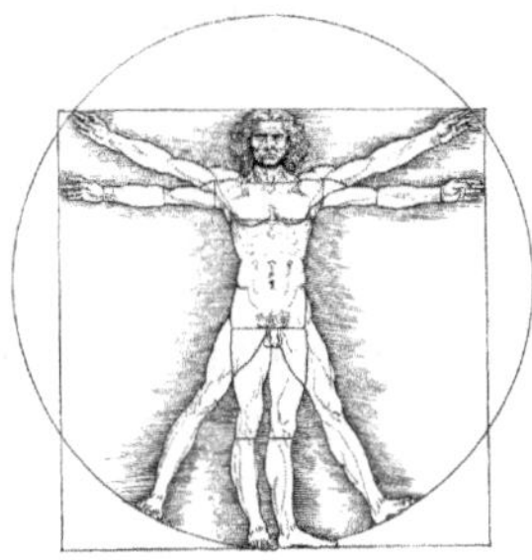

Da Vinci's Vitruvian Man (c. 1490) isn't a yoga concept either, but I like his idea that the human body is a microcosm of the universe. Plus, he kind of looks like he could be on a yoga mat. For Da Vinci, the circle symbolizes the divine and the heavens, while the square represents the earth and the physical world. The fact that the figure fits perfectly inside both shapes suggests a deep connection between the human and the divine — and that the body itself reflects the order and harmony of the universe.

Yoga plugs you straight into that same intersection. Every session starts (and ends) in a grounded, gravity-bound position on your mat, focused on your breath. Finding stillness can be a welcome relief or a surprisingly difficult challenge, depending on the day. Regardless of where you start, yoga gives you a real-time dashboard of your complete Sovereignty Triangle — mind, body, and spirit — allowing you to access and influence their state in the moment.

Yoga tunes you into your whole body

Yoga tunes you into your whole body in a way few practices can. It functions as both a powerful exercise system and a real-time personal dashboard for your SPiCE reserves — giving you immediate, honest feedback on the state of your mind, body, and spirit.

Through mindful movement and breath you gain strength, flexibility, balance, and pain relief in the **Physical** pillar. The **Intellectual** pillar sharpens with improved focus and mental clarity as you quiet the constant chatter in your mind. The **Emotional** pillar builds resilience and steadiness, while the **Spiritual** pillar opens the door to inner peace, gratitude, and connection to something larger. Even the **Currencies** pillar grows richer through the sense of community and deeper relationships formed on the mat.

Tom M., at 62 with more than eleven years of practice, captured it well: "I would say it has helped me most with my mental focus, emotional resiliency, and ability to concentrate, and to push myself past when I consider my physical limitations. Physically, it has helped me reduce my pain and improve my overall health; and spiritually, I find I am much more in touch with my emotions after I practice my yoga."

This heightened body awareness — noticing every stretch, contraction, release, and breath — becomes a living metric you carry into daily life, improving posture, reducing stress, and strengthening the mind-body-spirit connection that supports your entire second act.

Final Thoughts

Yoga's positive effects are not limited to any one aspect; they are deeply interrelated and interconnected. What began as a search for renewal across mind, body, and spirit finds its highest expression in three quiet but powerful forces.

Gratitude is the secret to happiness — it's not the other way around. Yoga gives you the space and the tools to cultivate that spirit of gratitude every single time you step on the mat.

Right there beside it sits its steady partner: equanimity. That even-tempered steadiness Rex nailed in one word — the pharmaceutical-free anxiety neutralizer that lets you accept both the good and the difficult without being knocked off center.

And anchoring them both is a resilient body — strong, balanced, and finally at home in its own skin. Yoga trains you to move both with and against gravity, to build real strength and flexibility that lasts, and to feel your body as a trusted ally rather than a burden or an afterthought.

Together they deliver the full mind-body-spirit promise of this ancient system: a **grateful heart** that stays open, an **equanimous mind** that stays steady, and a **resilient body** that feels strong, balanced, and truly at home in its own skin. Ten-plus years later, I still step on my yoga mat and feel all three rising — the same way my footprints and handprints keep building on it like a living time-lapse film, a tangible space-time emulsion that serves as visible proof that real renewal is happening.

That's why yoga remains the single most powerful fulcrum I discovered. It is an ancient system that delivers modern sovereignty — mind, body, and spirit working together instead of being outsourced or run on default settings.

Ancient system. Modern wisdom. Your second act deserves nothing less.

Chapter Seven

Best Practices: Reset Your Mindset

"I wish I dared to live a life true to myself, not the life others expected of me."
—The #1 regret of the dying

Now that you've begun to name your ERGO Purpose and started to perhaps ponder your image versus identity, it's time to reset your mindset before the real work begins. Not living a life true to oneself was the number one regret of the dying, as recorded by Bronnie Ware, a palliative nurse who kept a running list throughout her 30-year career in her book "*The Top Five Regrets of the Dying.*" That's why "Be Authentic" is #1 on *Sabbaticaleer's* Top Ten Best Practices list.

A central goal of this book is to help you hopefully circumvent that fate.

To ensure the best possible return on your investment, an essential step in your pre-sabbatical prep is to reset your mindset before you go. To help you avoid potential pitfalls and frustration, *Sabbaticaleer* shares its Top Ten Best Practices to deliver a little sabbatical wisdom and help you reboot your head and heart and align your trajectory with success.

Sabbaticaleer Top 10 Best Practices

#1 – Be Authentic

There are few things more personal than a sabbatical. Fundamentally, it is about your growth, self-reflection, and realignment. Nowhere in your strategy or intent should there be an ounce of concern to please or impress others; it's about fidelity to self and your higher purpose. While *Sabbaticaleer* recommends seeking out and listening to trusted friends and advisors when considering important decisions, this is your time to self-reflect and identify your needs.

Fortify your foundation. Realign your trajectory.

Socrates told us, "Know thyself." *Sabbaticaleer* says to do that and more: *Know thyself...and aim high to be true to your best self.*

#2 – Leave work behind

The quicker you make a decisive break from work, the faster you're genuinely on sabbatical. Without a clear separation, your old job risks remaining a destabilizing center of gravity, delaying the multi-dimensional SPiCE reset you seek. *Sabbaticaleer* isn't suggesting you burn any bridges. It's simply encouraging you to recognize the importance of making a proper crossing. If you're returning to your company, build a structured temporary separation into your sabbatical strategy. Staying connected to an old job out of guilt or a sense of indispensability adds unnecessary stress. Rip that Band-Aid off!

On my first sabbatical day, nothing was more liberating than a palpable awareness of a new lightness of being, as if someone had lifted a heavy burden off my shoulders. That's what a true reset gives you: a new sense of freedom. Another significant benefit of making a clean break is that it gives you your first real opportunity to self-reflect on what brought you to this point with a measure of objectivity, not unduly influenced by your current employment.

Finally, a clean break is a good proof point that you are on board and understand what a sabbatical can bring to your SPiCE needs. It conveys to others and yourself that you're committed to this endeavor.

#3 – Set Clear Boundaries from Day One

If good fences make good neighbors, good boundaries make great sabbaticals.

The faster you establish and stick to clearly defined boundaries, the quicker you will enjoy the true liberation a sabbatical can provide. Without clear boundaries, you and those around you risk unnecessary frustration. That's wasted energy.

Understand that you are likely not taking your sabbatical in isolation. Unless you are getting ready to head off on a grand solo adventure, you will likely still be living in the real world with unavoidable responsibilities. You could still have family or other commitments that require ongoing attention or a plan. With that in mind, a sabbatical is not about abdicating your daily or family responsibilities. While I formally left my job, I was still a husband and father during my sabbatical, so my duties in that regard did not go away. However, I set and communicated clear boundaries of when I would be unavailable.

You may even have to fight for your sabbatical, at least for how you want it to be. Boundary areas might include *defining your availability* ("remember this is a job and significant investment for me, please respect my daily office hours"), *clarifying strategic priorities* (being clear helps avoid unnecessary stress), or *building balance* into your workweek (scheduling dedicated time for the needs of others or your household).

Avoid conflicting expectations. Set simple ground rules you can reference and use to educate those around you quickly. It's easy for friends and family to assume you have all the free time in the world for things when the reality is precisely the opposite. Remember what the famous Philosopher Coach Morris Buttermaker said: *"When you assume, you make an ASS out of both U and ME."*

Helping people understand that – in reality – you have a finite time to get a lot of heavy lifting done provides essential context. As the Boss, it's your responsibility to nurture and protect the space you require, and writing your boundaries down is an integral part of your sabbatical plan. Be prepared.

Clear Communication is the secret sauce for maintaining reasonable boundaries.

Establishing solid boundaries for yourself and those around you is one of the most critical steps to maintain your sanity and satisfaction during your sabbatical.

#4 – Create a sabbatical workweek and workday

Structure is critical to ensure you are efficient and productive throughout your sabbatical. Make time for all your SPiCE needs! With discipline, your sabbatical time can stay strong. Suppose you have heavy lifting to do on specific large projects. In that case, a defined workday and workweek allow you to build in time for exercise, meditation, self-reflection, reading and writing, and whatever else on your list that supports holistic healing. It will also give you the freedom, outside your workweek, to still do fun things with friends and family and continue to live an integrated life.

I was generally busy "at work" as a Sabbaticaleer minimally on weekdays from 8:30 am to 3:30 pm, intentionally paralleling my kids' school day. I wanted to be around to meet them at the school bus. But my sabbatical also involved a deep dive into cooking, so at many dinner times I was still technically "at work." And sabbatical activities often include weekends or extended trips away from home. Your definitions and details will dictate your approach, but integrating structure is what *Sabbaticaleer* is talking about.

Having a defined schedule was also the most crucial boundary with my spouse. After all, for the previous 25+ years, every workday began with a kiss goodbye, followed by about 10 hours of separation before returning home for dinner. Everyone needs space in healthy relationships. Work days do that; a sabbatical workday is a healthy boundary, not a foreign idea. It provides latitude to escape the house and recreate familiar routines both at home and away. Family responsibilities, like school meetings, were honored, of course, but otherwise we agreed that if I was "at home" during my "work day," it was not a time for her to expect me to tackle home projects or a "honey do" list.

Finally, build balance into your workweeks. A sabbatical should offer a balance between relaxation and productivity. By scheduling your activities and downtime, you can avoid burnout and ensure you return from your sabbatical feeling refreshed.

#5 – Decompression Time

It's vital to actively shift gears from your pre-sabbatical life of work and stress to find a renewed balance. Don't underestimate the value of some dedicated decompression time between your pre-sabbatical mindset and when you start. Day 1 of my sabbatical brought that tangible newfound lightness of being, but I was still fried. I needed a little time simply to veg out, heal, and spoil myself.

If you want some anecdotal proof of this concept, witness yours truly driving the 6 hours home after Christmas Holidays at my in-laws. It was my official first sabbatical day (I didn't count the holiday break), and it took less than an hour on the road to ignore one of my sabbatical goals: to slow down (and not just in my car). The State Trooper and that speeding ticket sure slowed me down. I had nowhere to be fast. The irony! But tangible proof I needed to decompress and get my head wrapped around the seriousness of the sabbatical and what it was about: my purposeful, personal realignment.

Undoubtedly, having a long enough sabbatical to build adequate decompression time into your schedule is a true luxury. The first month of my sabbatical, I dedicated myself to listening for clues from my mind, body, and spirit. During my decompression time, I focused on massages, saunas, and low-impact exercise at the gym, my new favorite place. Regardless of the length of your sabbatical, *Sabbaticaleer* recommends building in time for decompression and transition, in whatever form suits you, based on your pre-sabbatical circumstances.

#6 – Intentionality

Intentionality ensures that you have a clear purpose, stay on track, make the most of your time away, and ultimately achieve the personal and professional growth you seek. It's about being mindful and deliberate in your choices and actions during your sabbatical to maximize its benefits.

Intentionality helps you get the job done well. Intentionality enables you to define your purpose (see Chapter 3). Clarity of purpose ensures you avoid aimlessness. Intentionality keeps you focused on your goals, which holds your aim true. Intentionality helps you make the most of your sabbatical, enjoy your plans, and stay attentive to new opportunities.

Intentionality encourages regular self-reflection and growth, as well as the discipline to keep a journal and track your SPiCE metrics, so you can have a record of your epic journey. Staying intentional throughout your sabbatical makes your Post-Sabbatical transition smoother.

Intentionality keeps you on task with this whole list and helps you set the boundaries to make them a reality.

#7 – Embrace Flexibility

Don't be afraid to be flexible! Flexibility is directly related to improving your Emotional SPiCE score. Flexibility cultivates resilience and problem-solving skills by equipping you to handle unexpected challenges with a calm and adaptive mindset during your sabbatical and beyond.

Be open to changes and ready to adapt to unforeseen circumstances or opportunities that may arise during your sabbatical. In Chapter 9, we'll brainstorm your SPiCE goals and sabbatical activities. You will want to stay true to your priorities, and having a structured sabbatical plan is essential. However, it needs to be one that can bend rather than break when opportunities arise or unforeseen circumstances dictate. Periodically review and revise your plan as your sabbatical progresses. Your priorities and interests may evolve, so be willing to adjust your activities accordingly. And the reality is, you will likely encounter new opportunities and potentially balance them regularly.

Flexibility encourages you to be mindful and to savor the moments that present themselves during your sabbatical, moments you might have ignored in everyday life. While maintaining a focus on your goals is critical, don't be rigid in your approach to achieving them, lest you create unnecessary pressure. One tangible change I made on Day 1 of my sabbatical to encourage flexibility was to stop wearing a watch. Flexibility ensures you can pursue your purpose comfortably and at your own pace.

#8 – Stay Connected

Another top 5 regret of the dying identified by that palliative nurse was that they said: "They wished they had stayed better connected to friends." That's one reason *Sabbaticaleer* focuses on the importance of your Currencies as one of the five SPiCE pillars. We will discuss the rewards of this concept in greater detail later in the book, but suffice it to say that being connected versus isolated delivers significant benefits across various aspects of well-being, mental health, personal growth, and overall happiness.

Use your sabbatical to consider reconnecting with old friends. And lean into making new ones by exploring new communities. Maintain contact with loved ones to foster emotional well-being and share experiences with family and friends.

#9 – Plan ahead

As much as possible, plan your sabbatical to address logistics, finances, and any work-related responsibilities. You're checking the box if you're reading this book while considering a sabbatical. If you've started your journey already and feel behind, consider carving out time now to work through the Workshop Chapters of this book and make up for lost ground.

Planning for me also included talking to people I knew who had taken a sabbatical. That provided real-world context and experience that was always enlightening and encouraging; and it informed the basis for what eventually evolved into much of the Workshop chapters of this book.

#10 – Have Fun!

Last but not least, make it fun! Having fun is more than just a best practice. Having fun is a secret sauce that increases your overall SPiCE reserves. Fun is a stress reducer, and sabbaticals are all about helping you reduce stress and boost your mood. Fun is rejuvenating rather than draining, and it increases your chances of finding new roads of creativity and innovation. Sabbatical is your best job ever because you had fun getting all that personal heavy lifting and soul searching done.

You can be serious about your sabbatical and still have fun. And the lasting memories you make will center around the fun you had and achieving great things while on sabbatical. Having fun contributes to a healthy work-life balance, a great benefit of a life realigned for the long haul.

Post Script

In case you were wondering what the other four of the top five most common regrets of the dying were, they were:

- Wishing they'd worked less and spent more time with loved ones.

- Wishing they'd expressed their feelings more openly and honestly.

- Wishing they'd stayed in touch with old friends and made new ones.

- Wishing they'd allowed themselves to be happier and embraced life more fully.

Homework - grab that journal!

1. Do you have any current regrets that you'd like to address or neutralize?

2. How does practicing "Be Authentic" change the way you think about your image versus your identity? Where in your life are you still performing instead of being?

3. Which of the 10 Best Practices feels most natural to you right now, and which one feels the most challenging? Why? What small step could you take during your sabbatical to lean into the hard one?

4. Looking at your SPiCE scores from Chapter 1, which practice from this chapter could create the biggest positive shift in your weakest pillar? How might you apply it?

5. After reading this chapter, what is one mindset shift you want to carry into your sabbatical planning? How will you remind yourself of it when old habits creep back in?

6. Pick your top 3 practices from the list that made you think differently about successful sabbaticals. Why?

7. How good are you at creating and maintaining clear and healthy boundaries? Especially with loved ones? Think about how you can communicate this concept in a win-win manner.

Chapter Eight

Systems that Stick

"You do not rise to the level of your goals. You fall to the level of your systems."
— James Clear, Atomic Habits

The ten Best Practices in the last chapter are powerful — but they only become truly effective when they stop being good ideas and turn into repeatable systems you can actually live by long after your sabbatical ends.

That's exactly what this chapter is about.

You've just encountered a powerful mindset reset. Now it's time to turn those insights into the quiet infrastructure that keeps your second act on course. It's all too easy to walk away from a sabbatical — or a New Year's resolution — with a notebook full of great intentions that quietly fade once real life kicks in again.

That's not a failure of willpower. It's a failure of systems.

Why Goals Often Fall Short (and Why Systems Win)

I'm not the real expert on this stuff — there are way better ones out there. In the Image vs Identity chapter, I referenced a quiet commitment during my sabbatical: whenever someone I respected recommended a book, I would actually get it and read it. James Clear's *Atomic Habits* and Scott Adams' *How to Fail at Almost Everything and Still Win Big* were two of those books. The concepts they advocated made a big impression, and they're the inspiration for this chapter.

James Clear put it plainly: "You do not rise to the level of your goals. You fall to the level of your systems." Scott Adams says it even more directly: "A goal is a specific outcome you want; a system is a repeatable process that increases your chances of success over time."

Goals create what Adams calls "pre-success failure." Every day you haven't hit the target yet, you're technically failing, and that slow drip of discouragement wears you down. Goals also rely on finite willpower and all-or-nothing thinking. Miss once, and the whole effort can feel like a bust.

Systems are different. They give you daily wins instead of distant maybes. They turn good intentions into automatic behavior that compounds quietly over time. They shift your identity from "I'm trying to become the kind of person who..." to "I am that person because this is what I do."

Systems Create Sovereignty

A sabbatical is fundamentally about reclaiming ownership of your life. It's a deliberate reset or reboot away from the daily grind, giving you the space to see things clearly for the first time in years. Whether you're taking a restorative break to heal and recharge, pursuing a clear Objective like writing a book or going on a meaningful trip, or simply stepping away from the grind to gain fresh perspective, the deeper goal is the same: to stop outsourcing your mind, body, and spirit to external demands, fleeting motivation, or default habits. You take back sovereignty.

This is the time to evaluate what's working and what isn't — using the SWOT analysis from Chapter 5, the lessons from Knowledge vs Narrative, and the honest look at Image vs Identity. You begin to prioritize the activities, projects, and focal points that will become the seeds for future systems — or the systems themselves — that keep your trajectory headed in the direction you truly want.

Some sabbaticals focus on immediate renewal. Others plant seeds for bigger change. In every case, the time you carve out gives you the space to regain influence over your own trajectory. The repeatable systems you begin to build — or even just the perspective shifts you experience — become the quiet engine that turns that renewed ownership into a lasting second act.

Every time you complete a system you designed for yourself, you get a small but real daily win. That steady feeling of "I did what I intended" builds the kind of inner authority that no one else can give you or take away. It's how you move from hoping for better balance to actively nurturing it across every SPiCE pillar for the long run.

ERGO + SPiCE + Systems = Real Progress

ERGO gives you direction — the sandbox (or blend of sandboxes) you chose for your sabbatical. SPiCE gives you the measurable dashboard so you know exactly where you stand and where you want to shift. Systems are what actually move the needle on those scores and turn good intentions into lasting change.

The entire *Sabbaticaleer* process itself is a system: Your ERGO purpose sets your direction, SPiCE gives you the dashboard, and the repeatable practices you build become the engine that delivers real, lasting progress. This is one of the quiet insights of the whole book — you're not just planning a sabbatical; you're learning how to build systems for a successful second act.

Turn Insight into Routine – Three Simple SPiCE-Tied Systems

Here are three small, repeatable systems I built during my sabbatical that still run in the background of my life today. Each one is tied to a specific pillar and takes only a few minutes.

1. Morning SPiCE Snapshot (Spiritual + Emotional)

During my sabbatical, I committed to spending at least a few minutes with my journal every morning over coffee. I'd quickly rate my five pillars 1–10 (not that they changed much day to day, but sometimes they would) and jot down at least one or two sentences about what I noticed and why. No overthinking. Just a gentle gut check. It was an easy way to create a habit that took almost no time, yet it kept me honest with the SPiCE process and priorities I set up for myself. It also served as a good early warning when something was drifting.

For a new Sabbaticaleer who may or may not be comfortable journaling, it provides an easy on ramp to creating a new – and important – sabbatical habit

Now years later I may not write in my journal every morning over coffee, but the ongoing self-awareness I've built in is still there.

2. Weekly Currency Audit Walk (Currencies)

Once a week I take a 20-minute walk with no phone. I ask myself: "What filled my tank this week and what drained it?" I note the people, experiences, and boundaries that mattered most. This simple ritual keeps my relationships and time allocation aligned with what I value.

3. Evening Emotional Weather Check-in (Emotional + Intellectual)

During my sabbatical, before bed I'd write one honest sentence about how the day felt emotionally and what I learned. Some nights it would be three or four words. Other nights it might be a paragraph. The digital journal paid big dividends here because I evolved this into a short dictation which took the pressure off of trying to find the right words. The habit itself is what matters — it keeps you processing instead of stuffing.

A Tuesday, Two Years Later

Picture a random Tuesday morning two years after your sabbatical ends. You wake up, make coffee, and sit down with your journal for the two-minute SPiCE snapshot. You notice your Physical score is a little lower than usual because you skipped your workout twice last week. Instead of beating yourself up, you smile, write "back on the gym tomorrow," and move on. Later that day you take your weekly Currency Audit walk and realize a conversation with your daughter felt especially rich — so you make a note to protect that kind of time. In the evening you do your one-sentence Emotional weather check-in and realize you handled a stressful work email with more steadiness than you would have pre-sabbatical. None of these moments are dramatic. They're ordinary. But they're proof the systems are still working — quietly, steadily, in the background of real life.

My Personal Systems That Stuck (and Why)

The real test of any sabbatical isn't what you do while you're off — it's what keeps working once real life resumes. That's why systems matter more than goals. Goals point you in the right direction; systems are what actually move you down the road, day after day, long after the initial motivation fades.

I didn't set out to build a perfect list of habits. I simply started choosing repeatable practices that helped me reclaim sovereignty across the *Sabbaticaleer* Sovereignty Triangle: Cognitive Sovereignty protects my thinking. Body Sovereignty honors my physical vessel. Spirit Sovereignty reconnects me to what matters most.

Over time these systems aligned with my SPiCE pillars and quietly became part of who I am.

Chuck, my friend and Pastor, had this in mind when he wrote me the following prescription.

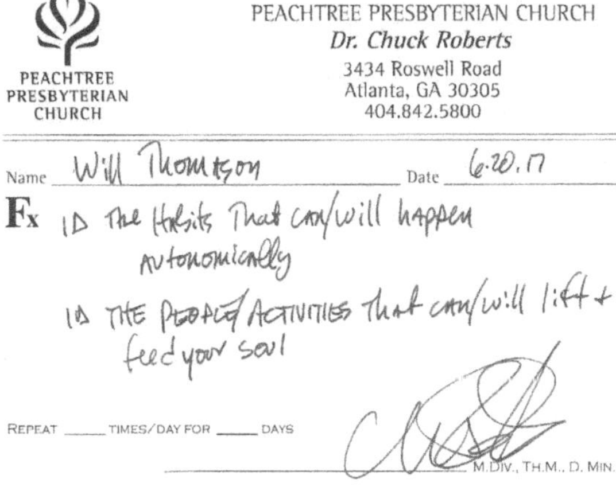
PEACHTREE PRESBYTERIAN CHURCH

PEACHTREE PRESBYTERIAN CHURCH
Dr. Chuck Roberts
3434 Roswell Road
Atlanta, GA 30305
404.842.5800

Name Will Thomason Date 6.20.17

Rx 1D the Habits That can/will happen autonomically

1D THE People/Activities that can/will lift + feed your soul

REPEAT ____ TIMES/DAY FOR ____ DAYS

M.DIV., TH.M., D. MIN.

Pastor Chuck's Rx for Resiliency

Here are some key habits that have stuck with me during and since my sabbatical.

At the macro level, my overarching system is my Christian faith and worldview. It gives me moral and ethical consistency, internal logic, and enough flexibility that it doesn't become rigid ideology. From that foundation flow many of the smaller systems that keep me grounded and pointed true north.

On a daily basis, the AM Reframe is one of the simplest and most powerful. By being deliberate about what I consume first thing in the morning — prayer or meditation instead of news, email or social media — I protect my heart and set my own frame for the day rather than letting the algorithm (or others) set it for me. This small practice supports my Spiritual and Emotional pillars and quietly builds Cognitive Sovereignty before the world even wakes up.

Intermittent fasting (my regular 16:8 window plus occasional longer 24- to 48- or 72-hour fasts) has become a reliable Physical system. It supports autophagy, built-in calorie control, and overall health while also sharpening mental clarity and building emotional discipline. The practice gives my body a regular reset so I'm not at the mercy of constant eating or energy crashes.

My yoga practice, now well into its second decade with a minimum of three to four days a week, is the clearest example of a full mind-body-spirit system. It functions as my real-time dashboard for all five SPiCE pillars and has delivered steady strength, equanimity, and resilience that no one-time goal ever could.

Finding and sticking with trusted financial advisors to manage our money to allow me and my family to focus on the bigger Currencies in our life.

I also maintain regular medium-sized systems that nurture my Currencies and Spiritual pillars. Leading a table in my church's Ironmen men's group has given me seventeen years of Tuesday mornings with guys who hold me accountable, provide, community, and encourage faith-based growth. These like-minded men are my built-in 2 a.m. crisis call if needed. Staying active in couples community and church life with my wife, along with regular Habitat for Humanity builds, keeps me connected to service and purpose outside my own bubble.

Finally, a classic car restoration project I took on after my sabbatical has become an ongoing Intellectual and Currencies system. Working on that 1970 Mercedes with mechanic friends Ron and John — after my brother introduced me to them — has given me a living "use it or lose it" metaphor for my own original equipment while deepening family relationships and connecting me to a new community. You'll read more about that story in Chapter 10.

And there are others. But each of these systems — small, medium, and large — work together to nurture my SPiCE pillars and protect my sovereignty across mind, body, and spirit. They turned good intentions into a life that actually feels different, and they delivered the tangible results that achieved the sabbatical SPiCE goals I set for myself — getting (and staying) in the best shape of my life for the second half of my life, building steady equanimity and emotional resilience, deepening key relationships, and creating a clear sense of purpose that carries forward every day. The beautiful part is that none of them required superhuman willpower. They simply became repeatable practices that quietly compounded into something lasting.

How to Turn Any Sabbatical Insight into a Sticky System

It's simpler than it sounds. Once an idea sparks, use this four-step process to turn it from a nice thought on paper into something that actually becomes part of who you are:

Name the SPiCE shift you want.

Turn it into a tiny, cue-triggered, repeatable action.

Link it to identity ("I am the kind of person who…").

Build in a quick daily win and simple feedback loop so it compounds.

Do this consistently, and the insight stops being a nice idea and quietly becomes part of your daily life.

The Long-Term Payoff

These systems don't just help during the sabbatical — they become the quiet infrastructure of your second act. They keep your SPiCE levels from drifting back to your pre-sabbatical baseline. They turn good intentions into automatic habits. And they give you the steady confidence that comes from knowing you're no longer outsourcing your well-being to motivation or circumstance.

What one small system could you start this week?

Pick something tiny, tie it to one of your SPiCE pillars, and try it for seven days. Write it down. Notice how it feels. That single experiment is how real change begins.

Your Second-Act Infrastructure – First Seeds

You don't need a complete system list yet — that bigger, more creative work is coming in the next chapter when you brainstorm all the cool things you both need and want from your sabbatical. For now, just plant a couple of early seeds using what you already know from your SPiCE baseline and ERGO purpose.

Take a few quiet minutes and jot down your thoughts below (or in your journal). No pressure to get it perfect — these are just the first small steps.

Looking at your SPiCE snapshot, which pillar feels like it needs the most attention right now?

What is one small, simple daily (or weekly) action you could try that would support a positive shift in that pillar?

How does this action connect to your top ERGO purpose(s)?

One sentence on why this small step feels doable and meaningful for you:

Example: If your Physical pillar feels low, your seed might be "walk 10 minutes every morning after coffee." It connects to your Restoration purpose and gives you an easy daily win that builds momentum.

These first seeds aren't the finished systems — they're the beginning. You'll expand and refine them in the brainstorming chapter ahead and lock them into your Strategy Brief in Chapter 13.

Ready to talk about your sabbatical?

Now that you know how to turn insights into repeatable systems that actually stick, you're ready to take the next step. In the following chapter we'll dive into the fun part — dreaming big and brainstorming all the cool things you both need and want from your sabbatical. This is where the "best job ever" really begins to take shape, with no bad ideas allowed.

Get ready to let your imagination run free!

Chapter Nine

Time to Brainstorm your Sabbatical!

"The best way to have a good idea is to have lots of ideas."

— Linus Pauling

"Ideas are like fish. If you want to catch little fish, you can stay in the shallow water. But if you want to catch the big fish, you've got to go deeper."

— David Lynch

After Chapter 3's soul-searching and Chapter 7's mindset reset, it's time to shift gears and do some sabbatical daydreaming.

At its core, a successful sabbatical isn't rocket science—it's about aligning two things: **what you need**—clear, measurable positive shifts across each of your SPiCE pillars (Spiritual, Physical, Intellectual, Currencies, Emotional)—and **what you want**—the fun, meaningful activities and strategies that drive those shifts.

The best sabbaticals blend both. When your SPiCE goals matter *and* the activities light you up, the journey doesn't just fix what's broken – it reignites what's been dimmed. In this chapter, we'll brainstorm ideas to fill both buckets before moving on to filtering and prioritization in Chapter 11.

Think of your sabbatical as a diversified investment portfolio. Your five SPiCE pillars—Spiritual, Physical, Intellectual, Currencies, and Emotional—are the assets getting real time, energy, and intention. A smart portfolio doesn't bet everything on one stock, and neither should your sabbatical. Spread the investment across all five, so nothing gets neglected and everything grows stronger together. With time as your most precious resource, this balanced, SPiCE-centric approach turns a good sabbatical into the foundation of a high-return second act: more energy, clearer purpose, richer relationships, sharper mind, and the steady resilience to enjoy it all for years to come.

With a SPiCE-centric strategy, you balance your pillars—shifting what's low, protecting what's strong, and letting the natural synergies work—you create the conditions for long-term growth, realignment, and renewal that actually stick. That balanced approach is what turns a good sabbatical into the foundation of a high-return second act:

Brainstorming – What Success Looks Like

It will take some time, and that's by design. Brainstorming isn't a one-and-done sit-down session— it's a focused dump plus an ongoing conversation with yourself that stretches over days or even weeks. To get started, clear the table, and simply set a timer for 15–20 minutes and let everything spill onto the page without editing. Then carry that page (or a note on your phone) with you. Sleep on it. Ideas will keep bubbling up while you're driving, walking the dog, or standing in line for coffee. Jot them down the moment they hit.

There Are No Bad Ideas

Back in my agency days, we had one strict rule: There are no bad ideas in a brainstorming session! Worry about reality later. Write down the wildest, craziest, most impractical stuff right alongside the mundane ones. "Quit my job and sail around the world" belongs next to "take more naps" or "clean out the garage." Often the ridiculous, sideways ideas crack open new thinking and reveal pure gold. Don't censor. Don't judge. Just capture. The filtering comes later; right now, let the crazy ones breathe.

SPiCE Goals and Ideas – Two Sides of the Same Coin

Brainstorming is two sides of the same coin. One side is your SPiCE goals—the honest, measurable shifts you need. The other is the ideas—the fun, meaningful activities that light you up. They go hand in hand: needs shape what's worth doing, and the wants make the needs feel alive instead of dutiful.

Before you dive in, pull together what you've already done:

- Your SPiCE Snapshot – (Chapter 1) – your baseline
- Your completed (or close) ERGO Worksheet (Chapter 3) – your north star
- SWOT Analysis (Chapter 5) – your strengths to leverage, weaknesses to shore up, opportunities to chase, threats to watch
- Your Journal – your vault of insight

Keep these front and center. They're your compass.

Start with the Easy Ones – Let Clarity Emerge

Some ideas will snap into focus faster than others. Lean into the obvious first: the pillar screaming loudest from your SPiCE snapshot, the need that feels non-negotiable, the want that quickens your pulse. In my case, Physical lit up early: "Get in the best shape of my life for the second half of my life" anchored by returning to within 5% of my college weight. A yoga practice and a family trip out west quickly followed as multi-pillar strategies.

Those early anchors build momentum. The fuzzier ideas

Tips for a Successful Brainstorming

Print your progress and carry it in your back pocket. Revisit it. Circle favorites and focus on your thin SPiCE pillars. Give yourself permission to let it grow, shift, and surprise you. This multi-day process – intentional yet flexible – is where the real nuances emerge.

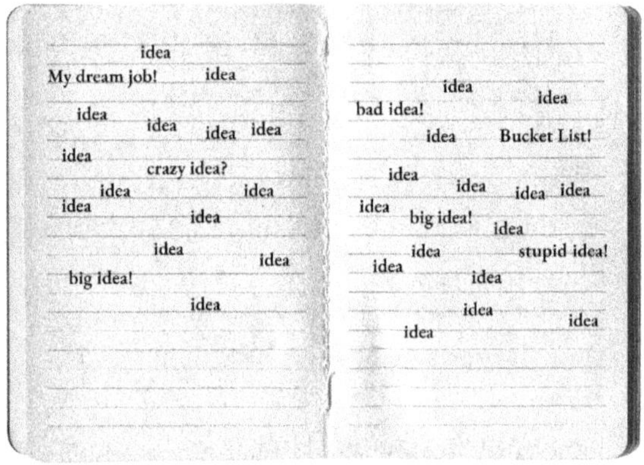

Brainstorm ideas for your *sabbatical itinerary* and carry them around in your pocket, leave them by your bedside.

Don't judge your ideas! Keep adding and tweaking. Sleep on it. Review and revise. Sleep on it some more.

SPiCE Goals vs. Strategies

Goals are the destination—the clear, measurable outcome you're aiming for. Strategies are the roadmap—the actions and activities that get you there. Together, they turn intention into real change.

As a frame of reference, below are the SPiCE goals (which aligned to my ERGO Anchors) that I developed for my sabbatical. For each, I had distilled down to two "headline words" as anchors and followed with short, tight statements that were intentionally action-oriented.

SPiCE Pillar	ERGO Anchors	SPiCE Goals
Spiritual	Reflection & Growth	Slow down, deepen my faith and establish a meditation practice
Physical	Restoration & Fitness	Get in the best shape of my life for the second half of my life
Intellectual	Exploration & Purpose	Create a purposeful life outside of the "grind"
Currencies	Realignment & Connection	Invest in what I truly value - existing, lapsed & new relationships
Emotional	Revitalization & Resilience	Create systems to live by to build long-term resilience; live in the present

My Sabbatical *SPiCE* Goals - yours will be different.

Be Honest with Where You Stand

Go back to your SPiCE snapshot. No sugar-coating. Challenge yourself to craft aspirational goals from that truth. Low Physical

– What would "best shape of my life" feel like, look like? Don't be afraid to face the cracks. You'll be better off when you fill them with sabbatical gold!

Non-Judgment & Acceptance

Observe your thoughts without labeling them good or bad. Some goals might feel selfish at first. Give yourself grace. Acceptance isn't resignation—it's the starting point for real change.

Identify your Tentpole Adventures

Sabbaticaleer calls them *Tent Pole Adventures*! These are the big, memorable experiences that become the structural backbone of your sabbatical. If you don't have one or two yet, keep brainstorming. They often need extra budget or scheduling thought, but they set the tone for the rest of the calendar.

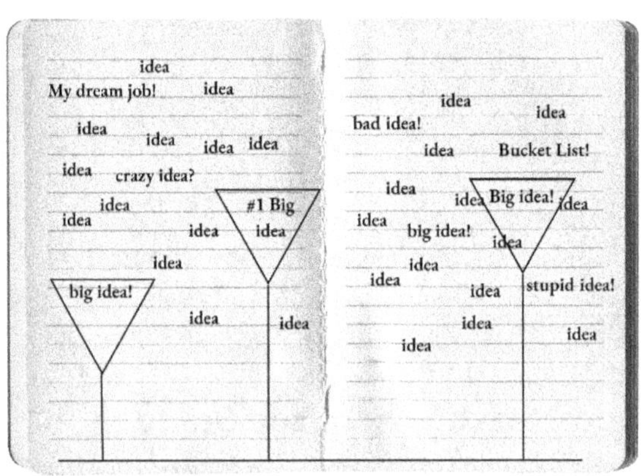

Tent Pole Adventures
Memorable focal points of your sabbatical

When you feel about 90% complete, pause. You're now primed to shape the the strongest ones into goals and ideas that serve your SPiCE needs and ERGO purpose. Chapter 11 will help you filter for leverage – how many SPiCE pillars each idea could positively affect.

You will naturally cull. I ended up with about 14 quality ideas and a range of medium and smaller ideas —a surprising majority got done in some form.

Brainstorming Questionnaire – use this for added traction

1. Easy Warm-Up (5–10 minutes – Start Here)

These quick prompts help you identify first anchor points without overthinking.

- Which SPiCE pillar is screaming the loudest right now? Why?
- What's one thing you already know you need to shift in your life? Why?
- What's one activity or experience you've been genuinely looking forward to?
- If time and money weren't barriers, what would you do first?
- If you could wave a wand and fix one thing, what would it be?
- Write down your first "anchor goal"

2. Deeper SPiCE Goals (10–15 minutes per pillar – Do One or Two at a Time)

Reflect on your Chapter 1 baseline SPiCE scores. For each pillar, name one primary goal (the big measurable shift) and 1+ secondary goal. Keep them aspirational but grounded.

Spiritual

- What's the biggest gap or opportunity in your Spiritual score right now?
- What would a stronger Spiritual pillar feel like in your daily life—more purpose, connection, or peace?
- How does this tie to your overall sabbatical purpose (from your ERGO ranking)?
- Primary SPiCE goal:
- Secondary SPiCE goal(s):

Physical

- What's the biggest gap or opportunity in your Physical score right now?
- What would a stronger Physical pillar feel like in your daily life—more energy, resilience, or vitality?
- How does this tie to your overall sabbatical purpose (from your ERGO ranking)?
- Primary SPiCE goal:

- Secondary SPiCE goal(s):

Intellectual

- What's the biggest gap or opportunity in your Intellectual score right now?
- What would a stronger Intellectual pillar feel like in your daily life—sharper curiosity, deeper ideas, or adaptability?
- How does this tie to your overall sabbatical purpose (from your ERGO ranking)?
- Primary SPiCE goal:
- Secondary SPiCE goal(s):

Currencies

- What's the biggest gap or opportunity in your Currencies score right now?
- What would a stronger Currencies pillar feel like in your daily life—richer relationships, better time ownership, or steady impact?
- How does this tie to your overall sabbatical purpose (from your ERGO ranking)?
- Primary SPiCE goal:
- Secondary SPiCE goal(s):

Emotional

- What's the biggest gap or opportunity in your

Emotional score right now?

- What would a stronger Emotional pillar feel like in your daily life—steadier resilience, more joy, or open-hearted flow?
- How does this tie to your overall sabbatical purpose (from your ERGO ranking)?
- Primary SPiCE goal:
- Secondary SPiCE goal(s):

Quick Reflection Across All Pillars

- My top primary SPiCE goal right now:
- How it connects to my ERGO purpose:
- Patterns I see (e.g., which pillar needs the most focus):

3. SPiCE-Aligned Sabbatical Ideas (10–20 minutes – Let It Flow)

Now flip to the "want" side. Capture any and all ideas – fun meaningful activities, habits, or experiences. Note the primary pillar it supports and any secondary ones. Use a simple table in your journal.

Quick Reflection on Ideas

- Which idea(s) feel most energizing right now?
- Which seem to primarily support your lowest SPiCE pillar?

- Carry these goals and ideas to Chapter 11. We'll evaluate them for leverage—how many SPiCE pillars each could positively affect—and start filtering the strongest ones into fulcrums.

SPiCE Goals and Aligned Ideas Worksheet

SPiCE Goals *What I need -* *Clear measurable shifts*		**Aligned ideas** *What I want -* *Activities & adventures that light me up*
	Spirtual *Primary* *Secondary*	
	Physical *Primary* *Secondary*	
	Intellectual *Primary* *Secondary*	
	Currencies *Primary* *Secondary*	
	Emotional *Primary* *Secondary*	

Quick Reflection Across All Pillars

- My top primary SPiCE goal right now:
- How it connects to my ERGO purpose:
- Patterns I see (e.g., which pillar needs the most focus):

Chapter Ten

A Sabbatical that Lasts

"The best way to predict the future is to create it."
— Peter Drucker

You've just generated a wealth of ideas and SPiCE goals — some practical, some wildly aspirational. Now it's time to step back and ask a deeper question: which of these will actually last?

This chapter is about what can happen long after the official sabbatical ends.

Four years later I still feel it every time I drop the top and pull out of the driveway. The engine note is smooth and strong, the original MB-Tex warm from the Georgia sun, and the wind rushes in exactly the way it did on that first drive in September 2022. This car — this 1970 Mercedes-Benz 280SL Pagoda — is living proof that a sabbatical can keep paying dividends long after the official time off ends.

The workshop chapters of this book give you the tools — SPiCE, ERGO, Metrics, Fulcrums, and a Strategy Brief — to plan and launch a sabbatical that resets your trajectory. But the real magic happens later, when the official time off is over, and you're back in "real life." That's when you discover whether the systems you built actually stick.

This chapter is living proof of what happens when they do. It's my story of how one post-sabbatical project tangibly delivered on the SPiCE goals I had set for myself and the systems I had put in place.

Look what I found!

It was Mother's Day 2022 when I discovered a barn find for the ages. Half-buried and hidden in a cramped and dirty garage for 35 years lay automotive gold. And I didn't have to go far. Right across the street from our home, our recently widowed neighbor, Hy, was starting to clean house, including potentially having "three old clunkers" towed to the dump to make room for her Honda. That day, as I walked up our street with her and my black lab Hunter, she casually mentioned they included an old Mercedes sedan (a 1959 Mercedes-Benz 220S Ponton), an old British sports car (a 1963 Austin-Healey 3000 Mark III), and a 1970 Mercedes-Benz 280SL convertible that her husband Bob had bought new when they were newlyweds. In the 20+ years we had been neighbors, they had never seen the light of day. Sight unseen, I expressed interest in the convertible only to have my hopes quickly dashed. She said our neighbor, Galen, had offered to help her unload the cars and that someone was already interested. But she added, if that didn't work out, it was all mine.

I got home and told my wife the crazy story of what might have been. She knew I had always wanted a convertible. Plus, we live in Georgia, home of nearly year-round convertible weather!

To her credit and my surprise, she told me to text Galen immediately and let him know I was interested. She said I'd regret it if I didn't. The text was sent ten minutes later, and I waited. The long and short of it: Galen said he was sure Bob would've wanted his long-time neighbor to have it rather than some random guy in California. He'd call his friend back with the bad news. And, with that, four flat tires were in motion!

With Hy on Day 1

This was all new to me, but my brother Dave has an old Merc, and more importantly, a trusted mechanic named Ron who agreed to meet me at Hy's to check out my find. Ron has been working on Mercedes for more than 50 years, so he knows a thing or two. Together, we removed piles of debris to reveal a dirt-encased 1970 Light Ivory 4-speed Mercedes-Benz 280SL.

Up to John's Specialty Repair! – May 31

It was obvious the car hadn't run for at least 35 years, probably longer. A 1987 registration sticker clung to its Georgia tag, but Hy recalled Bob searching for answers for years before finally giving up and parking it where we found it. He had built the garage to work on his beloved cars, but that love went unfulfilled until the day he passed on.

On a Tuesday, March 10, 1970, Bob purchased his dream car from RBM of Atlanta with an assistant professor's salary and a three-year bank note. Hy recalled an $8,000 price tag. Fifty-two years, two months, and twenty-nine days later, I became the grateful steward of a classic. A filthy, dirty classic. It looked like Pig Pen from Charlie Brown! Dust and dirt swirled from behind as I followed the tow truck as it headed up the highway to John's Specialty Repair.

The VIN tells us she was the 14,798th 280SL off the line of 23,885, of which about 13,000 were destined for the US. My own research pegs 85% were equipped with automatic transmissions. but Bob had custom-ordered his as a 4-speed manual, so I'm in the lucky 15%. He also ordered it without the standard Becker radio so he could have an at-the-time state-of-the-art cassette stereo installed before the US-spec'd *Frigiking* AC was mounted under the dash by the dealer. Ironically, getting that radio out proved to be one of the hardest tasks of all, but we're getting ahead of ourselves.

This was my first classic car, and I had a lot to learn. Up until this point, my experience had been with a long line of dependable Japanese brands — Honda, Toyota, Lexus. Dependable for sure, but not sexy. Certainly not inspiring or head-turning. I quickly learned that driving any of those modern cars grants you the superpower of invisibility. But driving this Paul Bracq designed SL? The superpower flips, and you get an instant taste of celebrity. Expect stares and smiles, and personal interactions at stoplights and in parking lots alike. It's a rare day that it doesn't spark joy in one form or another, not to mention outright gratitude for keeping this living time-capsule on the road.

My mechanical education began with John, Ron, and me sitting at the shop and agreeing on a plan of action. John explained that Specialty Repair could fix my car, but his business was not built around restoring cars except in the mechanical sense; however, they shared my excitement about my incredible good fortune and our pending mutual adventure. John has his own 250SL gathering dust in his shop so they knew the car well. We agreed to focus on dependability, system by system, so she could be a confident daily driver once again. I would clean her up, but returning her to peak driving performance — that was our objective.

There are a lot of reasons to love this car: its timeless design and state-of-the-art technology for its day. But for me, it's more than that. The W113 chassis, itself born to replace a classic, was built from 1963 to 1971. I was born in 1965, right at the height of this model's run. I love how it evokes the optimism and jet-age curves of what's possible. The 280SL screams '60s elegance: sleek, flowing lines, chrome, and a concave hardtop that gives the Pagoda its nickname. Its successor, the R107, is also a beauty, but conveys a distinctly different, injected-molded-plastic aesthetic of a '70s cruiser, prepping for highway comfort and the future restraints of imposed CAFE and safety standards.

Cars like my Pagoda come from an era that still inspired and reflected a feeling of what could be. That's the basis of its ongoing appeal: *an old car that still evokes a brighter future*. I embraced this as a metaphor for my own life and my sabbatical SPiCE goal of the renewal of my own original components (OEM in car parlance).

You quickly learn that a classic car is like the human body — a collection of integrated systems that must be finely tuned to work together. And like a murder mystery, we performed an autopsy for my long-hibernating Pagoda; we were essentially doing the same thing doctors do on a human patient: opening her up, system by system, to see what had failed. The fuel system is your digestion and energy supply, the oil system is your circulation and joint lubrication, the cooling system is your ability to regulate stress and recover, the electrical system is your nervous system and personal vitality, the exhaust system is your capacity to release what no longer serves you, and the brakes and steering are your emotional regulation and decision-making. Neglect any one of them and the whole machine begins to degrade — the same way skipping movement, sleep, or proper fuel slowly runs you down. Our two jobs were clear: fix her comprehensively so everything would run strong again; and identify the specific culprits that had finally sidelined her.

The Beauty of *Sabi* – Embracing the Marks of Time

There's a lovely cultural echo in all of this. The car itself is nicknamed a "Pagoda" because its slightly curved hardtop resembles the slanted, layered roofs of traditional Japanese pagodas. Though beautifully designed, the roof was engineered to provide enhanced strength and visibility — real performance benefits that improved the driving experience. That name feels almost poetic now, because a philosophy I embraced with my sabbatical also helped me appreciate the car's true beauty.

The technique of celebrating aged beauty dates back to the fifteenth century and is rooted in the Japanese philosophy of *Wabi-Sabi.* Kintsugi — the art of repairing broken pottery with gold — had already become a living metaphor for me during my sabbatical and appeared on the cover of this book almost from day one of my writing. *Wabi* speaks to simplicity, humility, and living in tune with nature. *Sabi*, on the other hand, celebrates the passage of time and the natural cycle of growth, decay, and renewal. It is the quiet beauty that emerges as things weather and age — the patina, the small cracks, the stories written into the surface.

As I built my SPiCE goals around second act physical and emotional resilience, the *Wabi-Sabi* angle dialed in even more strongly with this Pagoda. I was already philosophically aligned with the idea of pursuing excellence over perfection — which I knew to be unattainable. Budget certainly played a role, but it was really my philosophy that led me to hire mechanics to repair the heart and soul of this car system by system vs focus on an expensive facelift.

I have my brother to thank for helping me embrace the car's survivor beauty and appeal. A full restoration would have resulted in a beautiful but shallow result — the kind you can find in no short supply at car shows and auctions. Instead, by keeping its original patina while repairing its mechanical systems, we allowed the car's true identity to align with its external image — a car with a rich history of survival and now renewal. Of the roughly 24,000 280SLs built, estimates point to only about half surviving today due to accidents, winter salt and rust, and basic decay. People I meet are disproportionately drawn to the car's story of survival and rebirth as much as its classic design. I love that my Pagoda has such a unique story.

Sabi invites us to stop chasing perfection or permanence and instead find contentment in what is. It encourages us to see beauty in the ordinary, to embrace the transient nature of life, and to value authenticity over flawlessness. The faint scars, the faded ivory paint, its initial sixteen years as a daily driver in the Georgia sun followed by thirty-five years of deep dirty slumber before I rescued her — those weren't flaws to erase. They were the visible record of a life already well-lived. We focused instead on renewing what really mattered: making the mechanical systems sing again so she could find her true purpose back on the road.

That same *Sabi* spirit mirrored what I was doing with my own life. My sabbatical wasn't about becoming a shiny new version of myself. It was about renewing my original equipment from the inside out — healing, strengthening, and accepting the marks that time and life had left on me. Just like my Pagoda, I focused on authenticity and poured my energy into the systems that would let me keep humming with strength and joy.

In the end, *Wabi-Sabi* — and especially its *Sabi* side — became a quiet guiding philosophy for the whole project. It reminded me that real beauty and real strength often show up not despite the passage of time, but because of it.

The Renewal Adventure Begins

This was a car with a story: a story best conveyed through its well-earned laugh lines and wrinkles. Building on this originalist strategy, we decided to pursue, wherever possible and within reason, an OEM replacement parts strategy. What started with a leaf blower clean-out, and the stunning reveal of a first wash quickly shifted gears – an initial four-month journey to get her back on the road that was both intellectually and emotionally satisfying.

Fuel System

We started with the fuel system. After sitting for thirty-five years, the tank was full of rust and crud, the fuel pump was seized, the lines were brittle, the gauge sender was stuck, and the foam ring had turned to dust. We pulled the whole system and replaced it with a new tank, new pump kit, new hoses, new sender, and a fresh foam ring. The fuel system is the lifeblood of the engine. Without clean, steady fuel delivery, nothing runs right. Same as your own digestion and energy supply: if the lines are clogged or the pump is weak, the whole body starves, no matter how much you put in the tank. Fix it right, and the car (and you) run smooth and strong again.

Ignition System

Next came ignition. The old distributor was original points-and-condenser technology from the 1960s. We replaced the entire set — fresh plug wires, six new plugs, new rotor, cap, points, and condenser. Now she fires clean and strong every time. That's the spark of life. Let it sit too long and it loses its fire — same as us when we let mental chatter or distraction take the wheel.

Ron showing me the ropes

Oil & Battery

Murder-mystery suspect #1 emerged when we shifted to the oil system. Ron wiped his hands on a rag and pointed to the oil-covered valve cover. "Oil had spewed everywhere because of this scored crankshaft o-ring," which he handed to me as an early souvenir. After sitting that long, the oil was thick as molasses. He drained it, replaced the filter, and refilled it with fresh motor oil. At the same time, the battery was completely dead, so we dropped in a new one, and I bought fresh trunk mats to keep things neat. Oil is the lifeblood of the engine — it keeps everything moving and cool. And that scarred O-ring was just like a failing heart valve. The battery is your reserve energy. Let either one go bad, and the whole car sits silent. Same with your body: skip the important check ups and you risk not only a drop in vitality but also a a life-threatening breakdown. Keep them fresh and well-attended, and the machine will keep running strong for the long haul.

Brakes, Steering, Tires & Alignment

We moved through the rest of the systems with the same methodical care. Brakes got a new master cylinder, booster line, and four fresh hoses. Steering was completely refreshed with new tie rod ends, damper, drag link, seals, and belts. I made my first cosmetic decision here, opting for slightly larger black-wall tires that gave the car a more aggressive stance and more rubber on the road for safety and handling, followed by a full four-wheel alignment. These systems are your direction, balance, and stopping power. When they're loose or worn, the car wanders and you fight it every mile. Same as your own core stability and emotional regulation: when those are weak, life feels shaky. Tighten them up and everything tracks straight and true again.

Interior Deep Clean

We were (hopefully) approaching our first road test, so it was time to deep-clean the car. This was on me, and I spent all day at the shop with a vacuum, buckets of warm water mixed with Dawn, rags, mold killer, and 303 protectant, slowly peeling back thirty-five years of dust, dirt, and crud that had accumulated inside and outside the Pagoda. When I finally stepped back, the beautiful cognac-and-brown interior with its original MB-Tex was revealed — still rich, still intact, and far more handsome than I had dared to hope.

Air Conditioner & Cooling System

We made one deliberate compromise with originality to enhance performance. Under the hood we modernized the cooling system with a new A/C kit and water pump, plus a full radiator flush. The old piston pump was notoriously inefficient, sucking serious horsepower from the engine; we replaced it with a much more efficient rotary motor. The original Frigiking unit under the dash stayed exactly as it was. I don't use the AC often, but when I do it works great. The cooling system is your body's temperature control. When it's weak or inefficient, everything inside gets hot and miserable under load. Same as us — skip the systems that keep you cool under pressure, and you overheat fast.

Fuel Injection System – A Murder Mystery Solved!

The fuel injection pump turned out to be the real culprit all along — the center of the mystery that killed the car back in the early '80s and stayed hidden until we opened her up. Ron handed it to me and we inspected the damage. He said, "Mercedes and Bosch designed the first mechanical fuel injection system for these cars — it was cutting-edge at the time, a fine-tuned masterpiece that precisely measured and delivered exactly the right amount of fuel to each cylinder at exactly the right moment. When it's working right, the engine delivers peak performance."

Mine had three out of six fuel elements seized solid from rust. This was the one repair Ron couldn't handle himself. We shipped the pump out for a full rebuild and recalibration. When it came back, we paired it with a fresh set of fuel injectors, and just like that the mystery was solved and the car's signature growl was restored.

One final but fascinating parallel between this car and your body: that fuel injection pump is like your pancreas. Both are quiet, precise regulators that have to deliver exactly the right amount at exactly the right moment, thousands of times a minute. When they're healthy and properly calibrated, the whole system runs strong and efficiently. When they're not, the entire machine starts to suffer, no matter how much you work on the other parts. That's why rebuilding and recalibrating that pump felt like the single most important repair of the whole project — the one that finally let everything else shine.

First Drive! September 14

Three months and fourteen days later, we got her back on the road for the first time in over 35 years! She still sounded a bit like an angry lawnmower (new exhaust system and muffler still to come), but the engine was running smoothly thanks to all of Ron's knowledge and sweat equity – and of course that rebuilt fuel injection pump. Ron was straightforward about it: "She's only gonna drive better the more you drive her. And don't be afraid to push her." These cars were made for the road, and mine had been dreaming of it for decades. I was happy to oblige.

This was only the first chapter in her repair odyssey. There was still a lot to do. But that's what its all about. And today, thanks to all involved, I'm happy to report that I'm the proud owner of a mechanically sound, high-performance daily driver Pagoda.

With Ron and John

The SPiCE Dividends – Still Paying Today

Four years later the dividends are still arriving in quiet, steady ways. First of all, I drive it almost every day — unless there's a chance of rain or it's under 45 degrees. That's because I'm a top-down, all-the-time driver when I'm in my Pagoda.

On Monday mornings especially, as I head to the gym for yoga, I'll remember the man I was before the sabbatical — drained, stiff, and running on empty. Now I'm literally headed north up one of my favorite roads in a car that represents everything I built into my sabbatical. My body moves with strength and balance I didn't have since my thirties, if even then. My energy doesn't crash mid-day. My back doesn't tighten up after a long haul. The car itself has become a rolling reminder of the systems I put in place: yoga for resilience, better fuel for the body, clear boundaries for the mind, and the daily decision to keep moving instead of sitting still.

My **Intellectual** pillar stays lit every time I open the fat notebook that records every repair, every lesson, every dime spent. I've become an expert at finding the parts we need to keep her in top shape. My **Currencies** pillar is richer because of regular car updates Dave and I share over the phone, over lunch, or on weekends at car shows, plus the genuine friendships with Ron and John, who feel like family now.

Ron's constant reminder — "She's only gonna drive better the more you drive her" — became my own mantra and yardstick for my **Physical** pillar. The Pagoda was never meant to sit pretty on a trailer; it was built to be driven, pipes cleared, carbon burned out, every seal and joint kept alive through regular use. Same with me. During and after my sabbatical I repaired and rebuilt my original equipment from the inside out — yoga, movement, better fuel, and fixing my deviated septum — with the goal of building resilience and strength for the long haul of my own second act.

Emotionally, the payoff is pure gratitude — the simple joy of turning the key and knowing I am stewarding something well. That payoff felt complete last year at the local 5th Annual Deutsche Klassic car event. Dave and I recently attended for the fourth time. My Pagoda's story lives on two posters that outline the amazing before-and-after renewal and repair journey. The car is a stunner, but what people love most is the story. Last year my Pagoda was rewarded with the People's Choice award for Best Mercedes.

With my brother Dave at the Deutsche Klassic

That's exactly the kind of unexpected dividend you hope for when you build a Strategy Brief with honest SPiCE goals at the center. The sabbatical itself may have ended, but the systems keep working. And now this classic car — this living time capsule — carries the added gift of legacy. One day it can be handed down to my kids, who got to learn how to drive a manual transmission car in a 55-year-old 1970 Pagoda — awesome!

The Daily Driver Philosophy ("Use It or Lose It")

There's a hard lesson built into both old cars and the human body. The Pagoda was never meant to sit pretty on a trailer; it was built to be driven. Ron's constant reminder: "She's only gonna drive better the more you drive her." Floor it on the highway to clear the pipes, burn out the carbon, keep everything alive. Trailer queens look flawless outside but suffer inside from lack of use. Same with us — sit around, skip the movement or the systems you built during sabbatical, and the body (and spirit) degrades no matter how much surface polish you add. You rebuild your own OEM the same way: no shortcuts, just real internal work that keeps paying off.

Final Thoughts

Now, four years later, as I'm cruising with the top down on a perfect Georgia afternoon, it hits me: this car, this friendship with Ron and John, this deeper bond with my brother — none of it happened during my sabbatical. It all grew out of the healthy SPiCE goals I set and the systems I put in place while I had the time and space to think clearly. The sabbatical itself may have ended on paper, but the real work — the second act — is still unfolding.

I'm just a grateful steward of this living time capsule, the same way I'm a steward of my own original equipment. I keep the systems tuned, top-down, and drive her every day possible. I let it remind me that a well-planned sabbatical doesn't stop when you go back to work. It keeps delivering — in quiet joy, stronger relationships, sharper curiosity, and the steady confidence that comes from knowing you did the internal work when it mattered most.

If you *aim high from solid ground* – with a rebuilt foundation and reset trajectory – the dividends continue to follow. And, exactly the kind of second act you can create for yourself.

That's what being a true Sabbaticaleer is all about.

Chapter Eleven

Filter your Fulcrums

"A good system shortens the road to a goal."
— Ralph Waldo Emerson

Don't worry if your brainstorming from Chapter 9 is still percolating—this is an iterative process that can continue up to and through your sabbatical start. But with a bucket of raw ideas and goals in hand, it's time to start filtering them for leverage and get a glimpse of what a strong sabbatical plan might look like for you.

The final steps are to identify your *Fulcrums*—the high-impact activities that intersect with your SPiCE goals—and assess whether your budgeted time is adequate to make them happen. *Fulcrums* borrow from physics: a central leverage point that multiplies force across multiple objectives. In your sabbatical, they're the power cells—ideas that simultaneously feed and fuel multiple SPiCE facets (Spiritual, Physical, Intellectual, Currencies, Emotional) at one time. This step helps you strategically prioritize, building a holistic, balanced itinerary for optimized realignment and growth.

Once your *Fulcrums* are sorted, you can map how they work together and spot any gaps needing extra effort.

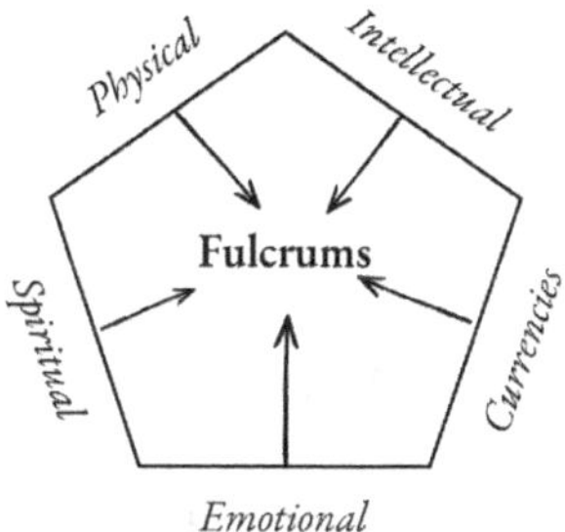

Your Fulcrums

High-impact activities that intersect with your SPiCE goals

Your Fulcrums are the power source for your sabbatical because they represent multidimensional ideas that align with your SPiCE needs. By clearly defining your SPiCE Goals and then identifying ideas that support them, you can organize and prioritize your efforts to achieve maximum holistic impact. *Sabbaticaleer's* experience shows that most ideas deliver on one primary and multiple secondary SPiCE pillars.

Why Fulcrums Matter

A sabbatical isn't about doing everything—it's about doing what counts most in the finite time you have available to you. Fulcrums are the key because they let one activity pull double (or triple) duty. In my 321-day gap, yoga became a fulcrum: primarily Physical (strength/flexibility), but it also hit Spiritual (meditation/centering) and Currencies (new community). That one practice amplified my renewal without adding extra load.

Step-by-Step Filtering

1. **Pull out your SPiCE Goals progress from the last chapter**

- As you filter your ideas, pay attention to ensuring your ideas deliver on your goals

1. **Assemble Your Brainstormed Ideas**

- Rank them from big to small. Circle the strongest ones that feel energizing and tied to your ERGO purpose.

1. **Create a SPiCE Intersection Table**

- For each idea, indicate which SPiCE pillars are impacted (primary & secondary) - Template at the end of the chapter.

1. **Tally & Balance**

- Assess how well they align with your top ERGO anchors and SPiCE gaps (from Ch1 snapshot). If critical gaps show (e.g., no Intellectual), add or tweak an idea.

1. **Sustainability Check:**

- Be real about time. How do these fulcrums align with your schedule? Build in buffers for rest and flexibility.

Here's what my Top 14 activities looked like prior to deeper planning. Each of these ideas delivered on at least three primary

SPiCE pillars, with three tentpole ideas eventually forming the backbone of my sabbatical.

Fulcrums Filter

Aligned Ideas	S Spiritual	P Physical	I Intellectual	C Currencies	E Emotional
Month 1 - Hard Reset, Decompression & Convalescence	Y	Y			Y
Gym schedule and Yoga Practice	Y	Y		Y	
Men's Mission Trip – first 1/2	Y	Y		Y	
Habitat for Humanity	Y	Y		Y	
Intentional Journaling & "Sabbaticaleering"	Y		Y		Y
Family Trip Out West – second 1/2		Y		Y	Y
Executor Duties			Y	Y	Y
Reward myself with a new shotgun and become a good shot		Y	Y	Y	
Less media more reading	Y		Y		Y
Become a quality cook			Y	Y	Y
Slow down, Be present	Y	Y	Y		Y
Faith Walk	Y			Y	Y
Purpose; Image & Identity alignment	Y		Y		Y
Invest in new communities	Y		Y	Y	
Totals	10	7	8	9	9

Tentpoles

- Tentpole #1 - A Mission Trip to Ecuador with my men's group from church primarily addressed

Spiritual, but definitely Physical (we were building homes for the poor), and Currency SPiCE needs as well. Locally, volunteering with Habitat for Humanity complemented this initiative.

Ecuador Mission Trip with Ironmen

- Tentpole #2 - A month long Family Trip out west leaned heavily into Currency (quality family time), but also Emotional (leaning into my own family after losing my parents) and Physical (lots of hiking, sightseeing, and rafting)

The Family Thomason on the Idaho River

- Tentpole #3 - Exploring a Yoga practice and developing a regular Gym routine addressed primarily the Physical (from rest to renewal), but also Emotional, and Spiritual SPiCE gaps

Filter your Fulcrums

Use the Fulcrums Filter at the end of the chapter to filter your Chapter 5 brainstorm ideas. Start with the 8–12 strongest ideas as a priority filter. But also don't feel as if you must limit yourself. I ended up with about 17 fulcrums of various shapes and sizes. Mark your SPiCE intersections (number of pillars hit), pay attention to ERGO ties, and rank by leverage (highest first). Ideas with true cross-SPiCE impact are your key fulcrums.

After you filter your raw ideas into a leveraged core, tally the balance and assess any major gaps.

Building Your Itinerary

With your fulcrums prioritized, you can begin to sketch a rough itinerary. Group into:

- **Big (tent-pole)**: Multi-week/month anchors (e.g., road trip).
- **Medium**: Weekly/monthly (e.g., yoga classes).
- **Small**: Daily/habit (e.g., journaling).

This isn't the final plan—that's Ch7's Strategy Brief—but it's the beating heart of a sabbatical that works. Keep the worksheet handy; the next chapter assembles it all.

Fulcrums Filter Worksheet

Aligned Ideas	S *Spiritual*	P *Physical*	I *Intellectual*	C *Currencies*	E *Emotional*
Totals					

List your ideas, write a Y under supported SPiCE Pillars, circle tentpoles, add up your Y's

Chapter Twelve

Envisioning Your Second Act with Legacy in Mind

"What you leave behind is not what is engraved in stone monuments, but what is woven into the lives of others."
— Pericles

You've done the hard foundational work — you've defined your purpose, brainstormed ideas, and filtered them into high-impact fulcrums. Now it's time to zoom out.

Before you lock your Strategy Brief in the next chapter, let's take a moment to look further down the road and paint a clear picture of the second act you actually want to live.

Wherever you are right now — whether you've already started building pieces of your sabbatical plan or you're still exploring the idea — this chapter is for you. Both paths are valid.

You're at the very beginning of figuring out your sabbatical strategy, much less the legacy you hope to leave. That's not only okay — it's exactly where you should be. Many of the deepest insights about legacy don't arrive fully formed on paper. They need the fertile soil and unhurried time of the sabbatical itself to take root and grow.

Why This Bigger-Picture Work Matters Right Now

SPiCE goals and fulcrums give you the "what." Your Strategy Brief, coming together in the next chapter, gives you the "how." But vision gives you the destination, and legacy gives you the deeper "why."

A sabbatical isn't just a reset — it's a bridge to your second act. This chapter helps you make sure the bridge leads to the right place.

Personally, I knew before my sabbatical that a clear pivot, realignment, and personal renewal were going to be critical if I was going to live — and leave — a legacy I could be proud of. I didn't know all the details yet, but I had an emerging sense of how I wanted to live my life: with *integrity*, *sovereignty*, *renewed purpose*, *deep connections*, and r*eal health*. On one hand, it was clear that without a sabbatical reset, those things felt out of reach. On the other, it was also clear that envisioning what those words put into practice provided a powerful North Star to carry forward.

Even if you haven't built your full Strategy Brief yet, or completed all the workshop exercises, this preliminary visioning will still give you your own powerful North Star to see what's ahead of you if you make the investment in sabbatical for yourself.

Get to Know Your Future Self

I learned the power of envisioning a future self long before I ever took my own sabbatical. Back in my agency days at 22squared, I was fortunate to lead a dark-horse pitch team going up against some of the biggest national shops for the Lincoln Financial Group account. We weren't the obvious favorite, but we had one idea that refused to let go: "Get to Know Your Future Self."

The entire campaign was built around thoughtful, hopeful encounters between people and older versions of themselves. One memorable spot showed a young father standing at the window of a maternity ward, gazing at his newborn through the glass. His future self — calm, gray-haired, and steady — stepped up beside him.

"Are you...are you me?" asked the slightly perplexed younger self.

"Yup", his future self replied, "in about 30 years."

Looking down at their newborn, the younger continued...

"So how'd we do?"

"We did great."

No big speech. No hard sales pitch. Just that quiet reassurance that the financial and legacy planning steps you take today are how you show up for the person you're going to become — and for the people who matter most.

We won the business. And two years later we won an Effie Award — one of the few advertising honors that actually measures business results, in addition to creativity. But for me, the real win was simpler: we had helped untold thousands of people pause long enough to picture a future version of themselves who was secure, at peace, and proud of the choices they were making right now.

It hit so hard and got so well known we won an even more highly prized accolade: it got spoofed on Saturday Night Live!

That campaign taught me something I still carry with me. Envisioning your second act isn't just daydreaming. It's strategic. It requires *Sabbaticaleer* Best Practice # 6 – Be intentional!

It's the same discipline I used to help brands win in the marketplace — only this time the brand is you. When you can clearly see the person you want to become, every decision on your sabbatical gets easier to make.

Envisioning Your Ideal Days

Close your eyes for a moment and picture a typical week in your second act. Not the fantasy version — the real, lived version that feels right in your bones.

What time do you wake up? How does the morning light feel in the kitchen or on the trail? What kind of work or contribution fills your days, and how much of it leaves you energized rather than drained? Where do you spend your evenings, and with whom?

If you're heading back to your current role refreshed, how do clearer boundaries and stronger SPiCE reserves change the texture of those days?

If you're stepping into a defined pivot or realignment, what new rhythms replace the old ones?

Try this right now — a guided future-self visualization

Find a quiet spot where you won't be interrupted for ten minutes. Sit comfortably, close your eyes, and take three slow breaths. Now picture a random Tuesday morning three to five years from now. Again, dispense with fantasy — you're seeing the real, grounded version of you after your sabbatical has done its work.

What does the morning feel like?

Spiritually, are you waking with a quiet sense of purpose and gratitude?

Physically, how does your body feel — rested, strong, moving easily through the day?

Intellectually, what are you curious about or learning that lights you up?

In your **Currencies**, who are you spending time with, what experiences fill your week, and what do you now measure as true wealth?

Emotionally, how steady and open does your heart feel?

Now zoom out a little. Look at the small, ordinary moments of that day — the conversation over coffee, the work you're doing, the way you show up for the people around you. Finally, ask yourself:

What one quiet legacy moment are you most proud of?

When the picture feels clear, open your eyes and write one paragraph describing that Tuesday as if it has already happened. Be specific. Be honest. Let it feel real.

Relationships and Community in Your Second Act

No one builds a meaningful second act in isolation. Who do you want closer? Which relationships need stronger boundaries or fresh investment? Where might new communities or deepened existing ones nourish you?

Think about the people who already feel like home, the ones you want to pour more time into, and the ones you might naturally drift toward once your SPiCE levels are stronger and your schedule has more breathing room.

Contributions and Impact – How You Want to Matter

What does meaningful contribution look like for you now? It might be in your work (whether you're staying or shifting), or it might show up in family life, creative projects, mentoring, volunteering, or simply showing up more fully for the people around you.

Tie it lightly to the SPiCE goals and fulcrums you've already identified. The activities that light you up are usually the ones that also let you give something back.

Legacy Thinking – The Long View

This is the gentler, deeper question: What do you want people to remember about how you lived?

Not the résumé version. The everyday version. The example you set. The difference you made. The way you showed up for others.

Take a few quiet minutes and jot down what comes to mind. No pressure, no performance — just honest reflection.

Bringing Vision and Legacy Together

Vision without legacy can feel shallow. Legacy without vision can feel heavy. When you hold them side by side, they steady each other.

Common traps to watch for: making the vision too vague or the legacy too burdensome. The sweet spot is a clear, lived direction that quietly leaves something good behind.

Your Second Act Vision & Legacy Exercise

Grab your journal or a fresh page. This is designed as a living document — you can come back to it during your sabbatical and long after.

Sidebar – This chapter reinforces the value of keeping a rich and authentic sabbatical journal. The truth is you will be doing this work throughout your sabbatical — and realistically long afterwards as well. Having a record, reference tool, and workbook on this subject will prove invaluable. And, creating a tagging system early in the process across topics and SPiCE pillars makes it super easy to assemble all the hidden nuggets quickly when needed.

1. **My Ideal Week** – Describe three things that would feel different (or the same, only better) in a typical week once your sabbatical has done its work.

2. **Key Relationships** – Name one or two relationships you want to strengthen or protect. What small, repeatable action would make the biggest difference?

3. **Where I Want to Matter** – In my work, family, or community, what kind of contribution feels meaningful to me right now?

4. **The Legacy I Hope to Leave** – When people think of how I lived, what three words or short phrases do I hope come to mind?

5. **My North Star Statement** – In one or two sentences, write the guiding idea you want to carry forward. Keep it simple enough to remember on ordinary Tuesdays.

From Vision to Action

You now have both the emerging vision from this chapter and the practical tools from the earlier chapters. In the next chapter you'll pull it all together into your strategy brief. Together they're a powerful combination.

Take what feels alive right now and carry it with you. Whether you're weeks away from your sabbatical or already living inside it, this North Star will quietly keep steering you toward the second act that feels unmistakably yours.

That's what being a true Sabbaticaleer is all about.

Power-Based Rebranding Tips for Your Second Act

These ten practical reminders, drawn from the same image-vs-identity work we explored earlier, help you translate your new vision and legacy into how you actually show up every day. When you're on sabbatical, return here and dive into a few as journal prompts and see where they take you.

1. **Excavate, Don't Fabricate** – Unearth your core values, strengths, and passions revealed during your sabbatical. Focus on self-discovery, not image manipulation.

2. **Vulnerability is Strength** – Share your transformational journey authentically. People connect with stories of growth, not polished facades.

3. **Ditch Limiting Beliefs** – Shed outdated self-perceptions like old clothes. Embrace newfound understanding with self-compassion and empowerment.

4. **Values Compass** – Define your guiding principles. Align your brand with what truly matters to attract like-minded connections.

5. **Integrity in Expression** – Ensure your messaging and actions reflect your authentic self. No promises you can't keep, no masks to wear.

6. **Contribute, Don't Compete** – Shift focus from

outshining others to offering value. Use your rebrand to share your unique perspective and contribute positively.

7. **Calibrate for Connection** – Elevate your consciousness to attract others on a similar path. Your radiance will naturally draw the right people in.

8. **Storytelling with Substance** – Share your sabbatical's impact with vulnerability and honesty. Let your narrative showcase your authentic evolution.

9. **Community Matters** – Seek connections aligned with your values. Find your tribe where your true self can flourish without needing to perform.

10. **Evolve, Don't Stagnate** – Rebranding is a journey, not a destination. Embrace continuous growth and allow your authentic self to guide the process.

Chapter Thirteen

Your Sabbatical Strategy Brief

"A goal without a plan is just a wish."
Antoine de Saint-Exupéry

You've done the heavy lifting.

You've honestly assessed your SPiCE pillars in Chapter 1, defined a clear ERGO purpose in Chapter 3, built your metrics and self-reflection system in Chapter 5, reset your mindset with best practices in Chapter 7, brainstormed goals and ideas in Chapter 9, and filtered them into high-leverage fulcrums in Chapter 11.

Now it's time to pull it all together into your Sabbatical Strategy Brief — a clean, one-to-two-page living document that becomes your personal GPS. This isn't busywork. It's the final strategic touch that turns your hard work into an executable plan, ensuring your finite sabbatical time delivers real, lasting renewal. Think of it as the final strategic touch from my ad world days: clear, integrated and ready to adapt as life happens.

Why a Strategy Brief Matters

In business or branding, a concise brief sets the stage for success; a sloppy one leads to wasted time and scattered results. The same is true for your sabbatical.

Your Brief gives you three powerful things:

- **Clarity** to execute with confidence
- **Accountability** through built-in metrics
- **Flexibility** to adapt when life surprises you

Beyond clarity and accountability, your Strategy Brief also gives you something equally valuable: a level of seriousness and professionalism that is important to several different audiences.

Professionally, whether you're returning to your current role or stepping into something new, having a tight, professional-looking plan shows you took the time to think it through.

For family and friends, it helps them understand what you're doing and why it matters.

And for you, it becomes a living document you can revisit throughout your sabbatical and beyond.

Step-by-Step Assembly

The good news? You've already done most of the heavy lifting in the workshop chapters. Now you simply pull it together. If you have any gaps, fill them now.

Your Strategy Brief is built from seven interrelated components. Try to keep it to two pages. Use the template on the next pages (or print from the workbook). Write in pencil or keep it digital so you can tweak it easily as your sabbatical unfolds.

Statement of Purpose

Write one tight paragraph that captures the high-level why behind your sabbatical — your ERGO sandbox (or blend) and the core shifts you're seeking. Pull directly from the work you did in Chapter 3. This is your North Star; everything else in the Brief should support it. Keep it simple and honest — no need to impress anyone. When you read it aloud, it should feel conversational and like the real reason you're doing this.

Your Current Situation

Summarize your "why now" in 3–5 honest sentences. Draw from your Chapter 1 SPiCE baseline and Chapter 3 SWOT. Be candid about what's depleted, what's strong, and what finally pushed you to act. This section grounds the whole plan in reality and helps you (and anyone you share it with) understand the stakes.

SPiCE Goals & Metrics

List the key measurable shifts you want across your five pillars, with simple ways to track them. Reference the baseline scores from Chapter 1 and the deeper work in Chapter 5. For each pillar, note one primary goal and any important secondary ones. This is where your abstract purpose becomes concrete — these are the numbers and feelings you'll check against as you go.

Strategies & High-Impact Ideas

Prioritize your top activities as fulcrums (starting with your tentpole(s) followed by the big, medium, and small) from Chapters 9 and 11. Group them under the SPiCE pillar each primarily supports, and note how the fulcrums that hit multiple pillars. This is the heart of the "how." Be specific enough that you could hand the page to a friend and they'd understand what you're actually doing.

Timing & Itinerary

Your sabbatical is a defined, precious block of time — your best job ever has a clock on it. Treat the timing and itinerary with the same strategic respect you'd give any high-stakes campaign. Map a high-level rhythm that aligns your big, medium, and small initiatives with your ERGO purpose and SPiCE goals. If restoration is your primary sandbox, you might front-load slower, healing weeks. If you arrive with a clear Objective, you might build momentum toward milestones. Most importantly, build in real-life buffers. Kids get sick, opportunities pop up, or you simply need an unplanned stretch to integrate what you're learning. Schedule regular SPiCE check-ins (every 30–45 days) as your built-in milestones. These aren't rigid deadlines — they're honest checkpoints to celebrate progress, spot what needs adjusting, and keep the plan breathing.

Logistics & Considerations

A beautiful strategy is only as strong as its real-world support. Take time now to map the practical side: realistic budget numbers (what you can truly set aside and where you might trim), work or family hand-offs, and clear boundaries you'll need to protect your time and energy. Consider any health appointments or routines you want locked in before you start. Think through communication too — who needs to know what, and how you'll handle the inevitable questions (see Elevator Pitch below – it will serve you well here). This isn't the glamorous part, but it's the quiet infrastructure that keeps your sabbatical from derailing. Get these logistics right upfront, and you free yourself to focus on the deeper renewal that actually matters.

The Legacy You Hope to Leave

In one or two sentences, write the legacy you hope to leave. Keep it simple enough to serve as your North Star.

Supplemental Elevator Pitch

Once your Brief is complete, *Sabbaticaleer* highly recommends crafting a short 30–60-second Elevator Pitch — a quick, clear summary of your "why."

Because you will get questioned. A lot. As soon as you tell someone you're taking a sabbatical, you can count on curious and potentially probing questions from friends, family, colleagues, higher-ups, and even casual acquaintances. Having a tight, confident answer ready gives you flexibility in your response. Sometimes you'll want to keep the conversation light and move on. Other times you'll want to go deeper with those who seem genuinely curious. Either way, the Elevator Pitch lets you choose how much you share while still staying authentic and focused.

The exercise itself is valuable too — it forces you to distill your sabbatical down to its essence and reinforces your own commitment to the journey. You'll be glad you have it during the planning phase, while you're on sabbatical, and long after it ends when people ask what changed.

Here's an example from my own experience (adjust the tense to fit where you are in your process):

"After burnout and family tragedy, I took a 321-day sabbatical to refill my drained energy reserves and realign for the second half of my life. I focused first on *restoration* — mind, body, and spirit — and then embarked on some adventures including a mission trip to Ecuador to build houses for the poor with my men's group and later a month-long trip out west to create an etched memory with my family. Recharged and refocused, I shifted to *explore* what might come next after leaving a successful but ultimately exhausting career in advertising. It became the foundation for this book and a much stronger, more purposeful, more satisfying second act."

Practice saying it out loud until it feels natural. You'll naturally expand or limit the details depending on the circumstances. You'll be glad you have it.

You're Ready

You now hold a clear, intentional plan that is unmistakably yours. This Brief isn't carved in stone — it's a living document, just like your sabbatical. Revisit it regularly in your dashboard.

You've done the work. You're ready to launch.

Your best job ever awaits.

Sabbaticaleer Strategy Brief

Staement of Purpose

Define your high-level sabbatical focus in one tight paragraph
Drawn from your ERGO work in Chapter 3

Current Situation

Summarize your "why now" in 3–5 honest sentences
Drawn from your Chapter 1 SPiCE baseline and Chapter 3 SWOT

SPiCE Goals

List the key measurable shifts you need across your five pillars, with simple ways to track progress.

Metrics

For each goal, note 1–2 simple ways you will measure progress (pre-, during, and post-sabbatical). Examples: monthly SPiCE check-ins, journal entries, or key milestones.

Strategies & Fulcrums

List your top high-impact ideas (big, medium, and small), grouped by the SPiCE pillar each primarily supports. Remember: Fulcrums naturally touch multiple pillars.

Timing & Itinerary

Map a rough timeline with built-in buffers for real life.

Logistics & Considerations

Cover budget, prep, boundaries, and any practical realities.

The Legacy You Hope to Leave

In one or two sentences, write the legacy you hope to leave.
Keep it simple enough to serve as your North Star

Remember: This is a living document to be revisited

Sabbaticaleer Strategy Brief – page 1

Staement of Purpose

Current Situation

SPiCE Goals

Metrics

Remember: This is a living document to be revisited

Sabbaticaleer Strategy Brief – page 2

Strategies & Fulcrums

Timing & Itinerary

Logistics & Considerations

The Legacy You Hope to Leave

Remember: This is a living document to be revisited

Chapter Fourteen

The World Needs More Heroes

"A hero is someone who has given his or her life to something bigger than oneself."
– Joseph Campbell

You now have – or are well on your way – your complete Sabbatical Strategy Brief in hand: a clear, living document that captures your purpose, your high-impact fulcrums, and your plan.

Before you put that plan into motion, let's lift our eyes outward for a moment and consider the bigger picture: the legacy you hope to leave and the quiet way your renewed life can become heroic for others.

The *Kintsugi* allegory in the Prelude that opened this book – as well as my *Wabi-Sabi* inspired Pagoda restoration, demonstrates that broken things, when repaired with care and virtual gold, become more beautiful and useful than they were before. A well-lived sabbatical does the same for you. It takes you wherever you are in life, the fractures, the burnout, the unmet needs, the untapped potential, the quiet unrest, and repairs them with intention — turning what was broken into something stronger, more radiant, and far more useful to the people around you. That is the everyday heroism this chapter is about.

In Chapter 8 we explored how the systems you build during your sabbatical can quietly keep paying dividends for the rest of your life. That brings us to the natural next question: once you've reclaimed your sovereignty and realigned your SPiCE pillars, what will you do with that renewed life? This chapter is about choosing to become a hero — not in the comic-book sense, but in the substantial, everyday way the world desperately needs right now.

An everyday hero doesn't wear a cape. They simply show up consistently as the best version of themselves — the parent who listens instead of lectures, the colleague who mentors without seeking credit, the friend who checks in when no one else does, the neighbor who helps without being asked. They reflect the inner work of a sabbatical so they can give their best energy outward. Their renewal ripples. That is the kind of hero the world needs more of.

##

I told you I lost my parents in a freak carbon monoxide accident in 2013. They had celebrated their 50th wedding anniversary and renewed their vows earlier that year. It was a glorious affair with family and friends in a community they loved at the same church where they were married five decades before. They were healthy and happy; six months later, they were gone.

That day was as bad as you might imagine. Friends of theirs called me early Sunday afternoon, worried they had missed their lunch date and were not answering their phones. Several days of stacked-up newspapers by their front gate and their cars in the garage added a sense of dread. I called my brother to ask when he last talked with them.

I called my uncle, who lived near my parents, and asked him to go over and investigate. He confirmed a worst-case scenario when he found them in their bed and unresponsive. They lived brain-dead for a week in the ICU as we dealt with this new and unexpected reality. That week, my brother and I camped out at their house, up late each night recounting our favorite family stories; we consoled each other as we drank deeply from Dad's liquor cabinet, toasting them as we did. We leaned into the love and support of family and friends. Then, thankful for the healthcare directives (Living Wills) they included in their estate plans, we gathered with family and said our heartfelt, emotional goodbyes before honoring their final wishes.

My wife and I made the decision not to shield our young children from the jarring reality of death. Our son was thirteen and stoic. Our daughter was nine and cried confused tears. I held my Mom's hand and told her how much I loved her; I read my Dad a letter of gratitude, saying the things out loud that guys seem to have difficulty finding the time, courage or words to say. Following their final instructions alleviated any guilt and made a gut-wrenching decision easier. Shock stifled my tears as doctors turned off their life support. Their bodies held on for a few more days, with my Dad dying the day before and my Mom dying the day after Father's Day 2013. He was 76, and she was 71. My Mom had made clear she wanted an Easter funeral. They got one, and it was magnificent, with a packed church, joy-filled hymns, and some bagpipes to boot. All my far-flung friends rallied to my side. And as my father taught me, stand tall and be an ambassador of the Thomason name in good times and bad. They were cremated and buried in our family plot at the church that was so integral to their lives.

We should all be as lucky as they were and spend a lifetime with our best friend. I am happy to report that I am nothing but grateful for the gift of having Bill and Woo Thomason as my parents.

As its title confirms, this chapter is not about death, dying, or losing parents. Most of us will experience losing our parents; it's part of the natural cycle of life. And we all will face death ourselves one day. However, don't take any life for granted, whether that be yours or the people you love. I'm proof they can be gone in an instant. Nor is this chapter about Carbon Monoxide accidents, though I've learned a lot about them; they happen all the time in various surprising and tragic ways. Invest in a CO monitor in addition to your smoke alarms, and make sure all your loved ones have them, too. They may be the cheapest life insurance you'll ever buy. Finally, this chapter is not about estate planning, though my brother and I are forever grateful that our parents left us a clean estate with up-to-date wills and clear healthcare directives. Ensure you do that for your kids and that your parents have them. It may be the most significant final gift anyone can give their loved ones.

Instead, this chapter is about being a hero because the world needs more of them — the kind of everyday hero your realigned second act can become.

Before you close this book, take a few quiet minutes with your journal or the back of your Strategy Brief and answer these three simple questions:

1. Looking at my SPiCE pillars today, which one do I most want to strengthen so I can show up more fully for the people who matter to me?

2. What is one small, repeatable way I can use my renewed energy to be someone's hero?

3. When people look back on my life, what three words do I most hope they use to describe the person I became after my sabbatical?

I loved both my parents equally, but I lost a hero of mine when my Dad died. Despite growing up without a father, my Dad was not only a role model to me, but also to many others because of the way he lived his life. Even though he wasn't a regular fixture in the news, he was a great example of a modern-day hero. Why was that? What can we learn about how he lived as a man and father that might increase our chances of being held in such high regard when we're dead? What will people say about you at your funeral to your family and friends? How would you like to be remembered? What will be your legacy?

First, can we agree that the world needs more heroes? Of course, some individuals occasionally break through the clutter in heroic ways, but they sure seem few and far between. When I turn on the news or check the endless feeds on my phone, heroes are in short supply. Our modern world disproportionately values iPhone-filming, social media-posting bystanders of chaos who record and exploit footage of civilization's latest embarrassment, outrage, or tragedy to feed a shallow, click-based dopamine habit. How often does the footage highlight individuals or groups stepping in to say, "Enough!" and saving the day? The answer is not nearly enough. In fact, to do so often invites severe penalty. These scenes are a grim reflection of what passes for institutional leadership in our country today.

It makes some sense, though. Leaning into chaos and being a hero is a risky business, whether online, on the front lines, or even standing in line, given the state of our world today.

This book has reinforced that your sabbatical is a pivot point, an opportunity for a rewrite, and an opportunity to consider the legacy you will leave. I'm here to encourage you to aspire for the heroic when considering your realigned post-sabbatical life. If not you, who?

And the thing is, heroes can take many forms across many classic archetypes. Some we get to choose, others may be thrust upon us. Maybe being the *Epic Hero* doesn't fit your current physique, but you can still manifest honor, duty, and sacrifice. Perhaps you fancy the role of the often-misunderstood *Outlaw Hero*, a rebel fighting for justice and freedom. Hopefully, you are not locked in the path of the *Tragic Hero*, flawed but noble, reminding us of the fragility of human existence. That can be tough, but if you're concerned that is your fate, you still have time to make amends.

As you take time on your sabbatical to refresh and reclaim your mind, body, and spirit and realign for the second act of your life, I hope you will recognize that you can make a difference and be the hero someone or some community needs. It can be a daunting thought! But there are accessible hero archetypes that the world needs right now that are available to you. You can become the *Wise Mentor*, an older, experienced figure who advises other future heroes through your wisdom, knowledge, and support. Or you can be the *Everyman Hero*, a relatable, ordinary person thrust into extraordinary circumstances who overcomes their limitations through courage and sacrifice. These last two archetypes were where my father shined, modeling a heroic life not just for me but also for those he encountered.

Of course, my father would never have described himself as a hero. But he would have talked to you about the importance of *integrity*, *inspiration*, *selflessness*, *courage*, and *perseverance*, and their power to make a difference in how you live your everyday life and positively influence the people around you.

What follows are five life lessons my father modeled for me and others, along with the impact they had. They are the words and actions of the Wise Mentor and Everyman Hero I knew as Dad, and of the one others knew across various relationships. They demonstrate that the leaders who make a difference and the heroes who inspire us do so wherever they operate. Each lesson quietly strengthened one or more of my SPiCE pillars and showed what everyday sovereignty looks like in action.

#1. Cherish your Reputation and Your First Impressions

It's fair to say Dad enjoyed an excellent reputation. Born and raised in rural Laurens, South Carolina, he became "the man of the house" before his first birthday when his father died, leaving his mother a widow to raise their only son alone. So, I think responsibility thrust itself on him from the beginning of his life. He accepted it and became a self-aware standard bearer of the Thomason name in all he did.

My brother and I grew up a world away in Bedford Village, NY, a 300-year-old hamlet an hour north of New York City. It was one step in my Dad's successful career and the first step in our upbringing. In Bedford, you only had to dial four digits on the telephone to reach your neighbors. It had no stoplights, and our bikes gave us access to all it offered. We enjoyed a freedom that seems all but non-existent for kids today.

But with freedom came responsibility. In whatever direction we ventured out, whether it was school, a friend's house, restaurants, parties, church, or anywhere else, he reminded us of one cardinal rule: Remember, always be a good ambassador of the Thomason name. It was either repeated aloud or understood to echo in the etched memory. And we fully appreciated there would be consequences if we let him down.

What started with the scaffolding of this simple mantra grew to encompass an expected standard of behavior, civility, and self-respect. It has served me well my entire life, and now as a parent of two children who have grown up with and benefited from the same cardinal rule. The genius of this phrase is that ambassadors are on the job when abroad. But at home, ambassadors of the Thomason name were still allowed to let our guard down. We were able to make mistakes, deal with the raw emotions of childhood, and blow off steam without fear of retribution. But away from home, it gave us a standard to aim for and something to be proud of.

He explained that there may be times when all you have is your reputation. So cherish it. Likewise, always pay special attention to people's first impressions of you because they are the cornerstones of your reputation. You only have one chance to make a first impression; don't blow it. Building on strength is much easier than repairing the damage.

My Dad taught me the heroic attribute of **Integrity**. Heroes know what they stand for, stick to strong moral principles, and consistently act with honesty, fairness, and compassion. They stand up for what is right, even when it is difficult. That lesson strengthened my Spiritual and Emotional pillars more than I realized at the time.

#2. You will make mistakes in life. How will you respond to yourself and to others?

I was in the 5th grade when my father's approach to dealing with life's mistakes came into focus for me. It has served me well ever since. It is "*the fridge incident.*"

After-school snacks in our house were a simple affair back in my day: Oreo and Chips Ahoy cookies. If you wanted anything fancier, you had to make it. Jello chocolate pudding was a favorite. Slice-and-bake cookies were an easy enough upgrade. On one particular day, I had a friend over after school, and we decided to make some Betty Crocker chocolate fudge brownies, which were quickly mixed, poured, cooked, and removed piping hot from the oven. So, they were way too hot to eat, and we were impatient ten-year-old boys.

My parents had recently completed a kitchen renovation, including a bar area and refrigerator for my Dad. It was their marriage's first big home project, so it was a big deal. And my friend and I came up with the bright idea of putting that hot pan of brownies in my Dad's brand-new fridge to cool. Minutes later, we removed the now-edible brownies only to encounter the price of our impatience: a warped, melted refrigerator lining and my abject horror at what I had done to part of my father's new pride and joy. My friend got home unscathed, but with my rattled nerves, I had to wait for my Dad to come home. Conversations with my Mom quickly boiled down to the reality that it was my responsibility to tell him.

He greeted me normally; I was shaking. I coughed up the courage to admit my deed. "Show me," he calmly said, and we inspected the bottom of the fridge. He was quiet for a moment that seemed like forever. I'm prepared for the worst, but he doesn't say anything. Instead, he motioned me to follow him over to our main refrigerator. He opened the lower freezer door. We crouched down, and to my amazement, he pointed his finger and showed me where it was melted on the bottom. I had never noticed it before. He said, "I did that, fixing the ice maker... I left my work lamp on when I went for a screwdriver."

With the "fridge incident," my Dad taught me the power of **Inspiration**. Heroes inspire others with their actions and deeds and, yes, even their mistakes. They serve as role models, showing what is possible and encouraging others to be their best selves.

I never really knew, but I'm sure my Mom called my Dad and told him what happened. I know that their actions and my father's reaction that day formed the foundation of my own approach to people's mistakes and parenting. Mistakes are inevitable, but how you respond to them doesn't have to be. As a brief coda, the fridge incident also represents, for me, evidence of God's work behind the scenes, a sign vs. a coincidence for those willing to pay attention.

That lesson strengthened my Currencies, Emotional and Intellectual pillars — teaching me that how we handle our own mistakes shapes the example we set for others.

#3. There's no I in "team."

This seemingly cliché truism was central to my father's leadership style. Nothing irritated him more than when people gave speeches or presentations overpopulated with mentions of

"I, Me, and My." Early on, my Dad taught me that both words and actions matter. Nowhere was this more evident than when he broke out his red editing pen to mark my college essays, where he taught me that nobody likes an egomaniac and that nothing says egomaniac more than overusing first-person references in communication. He would send me off to find more effective, less self-centered ways to discuss my ideas, based on his rule for communication and leadership: Never have more than one "I, Me, and My" reference per paragraph.

In college essays, a lazy reliance on "I, Me, and My" makes you sound repetitive, boring, and self-centered. At work, it makes you obnoxious and demotivating. The org chart identifies the boss, but Dad taught that words and actions define the leaders, regardless of station. Leaders have the confidence to act selflessly, willing to freely give credit to subordinates or the team, because they understand their job is to lead that team to accomplish objectives effectively. Conversely, the best leaders are willing to shoulder blame to protect subordinates and the team, which can pay big dividends in loyalty and enhanced motivation to succeed the next time.

My Dad taught me the heroic attribute of **Selflessness**: Heroes do not shy away from self-sacrifice. They sacrifice their comfort, safety, or potentially even their life for the greater good. They are team players, willing to give away credit and take the blame.

That lesson strengthened my Currencies and Intellectual pillars — teaching me the power of building real relationships through generosity and shared success.

#4. Surround yourself with people who lift you up and make you better.

For the past 17+ years, I've been fortunate to be a member of and lead a table at the Men's Group at my church called *Ironmen*. This community's name is inspired by Proverbs 27:17 — "As iron sharpens iron, so one man sharpens another." We meet at 7 am sharp on Tuesday mornings with well over 100 guys gathering around tables and meeting in fellowship to be inspired and inspire others. We end promptly at 8 am, recharged (and realigned!) to face whatever life has in store for us. Our mission is simple: To encourage and equip men to become a positive impact for Jesus at home, at work, and in the community.

I don't think my father was ever specifically aware of the Ironmen mission statement, but it was how he lived his life. He was an encourager, not a discourager, whether at home, work, or in his numerous communities. It is fitting that I've found a community that aligns with the principles my father modeled. A group of men with whom I share friendship and fellowship, and who have been instrumental in helping me navigate life's unexpected yet inevitable storms. My Dad always said that the people you surround yourself with will determine the trajectory of your life.

I was invited to my first Ironmen gathering to hear writer Gordon MacDonald speak at the now-defunct ESPNZone in Atlanta. I had never heard of him, but he had written two books I later read and recommend to you, *Ordering Your Private World* and *A Resilient Life*, and spoke before a packed room.

He recounted a story that hooked me on the idea of a Men's Group, especially one affiliated with my church.

The gist was that he had been speaking to a group of high-powered submarine commanders at Naval Air Station Miramar, where the original Top Gun took place. Offhand, he mentioned two types of older men: happy and grumpy. He said the secret to happiness was simple in concept: Happy men enjoyed authentic friendships where they risk sharing their struggles and weaknesses with friends they trust to call them on their BS. The grumpy ones were lonely or limited to shallow relationships focused on careers, golf handicaps, and the weather. Not only were these guys top-of-the-food-chain sub-commanders, but they were also expected to show strength, never weakness. They were on the road to grumpy and miserable, and they knew it. All their questions were about where and how to find such a cadre of men. They were high-performing Type A's operating in the dark, without a map, desperate to understand how even to begin such a mission.

I examined my life and knew what was missing. I was in a city where I didn't grow up or attend school. My childhood, high school, and college friends were great, but we were all scattered across the country. I lacked close friends I could trust, confide in, and depend on. I had a beautiful family and a great career, but the storm clouds were brewing. And like the sub-commanders, I knew the workplace was risky to expose weakness and vulnerability.

At that point, I confess I was still too concerned with appearances and my image. We attended church, but I remained insecure about broadcasting my attendance at a Men's Bible Study group to my highly secular advertising colleagues. But I ginned up the courage and had my assistant block out Tuesday mornings from 7-8 am Tuesdays. My Dad had taught me that leaders lead wherever they are and that integrity requires not compartmentalizing those efforts.

Ironmen has become one of my major SPiCE assets in my Currencies reserves with over 17 years of Tuesday mornings, not to mention a tent-pole mission trip in Ecuador and a decade of Habitat for Humanity builds. It provides me with friendships and fellowship with a community of like-minded men facing their own challenges at home, at work, and in their hearts. It's fair to say we know each other's highs and lows, prayers and praises, and struggles and successes way more than what we do for a living or golf handicap (unless we play together). We are each other's 2 am emergency phone call, a sounding board when critical decisions are made, and a shoulder to lean on during tough times. Even more importantly, Ironmen has encouraged me to dispense with my lukewarm, fair-weather faith and understand my role and responsibility as a man and a child of God.

I thank my Dad for teaching me the importance of **Courage**. Courage will always be the defining quality for heroes of all shapes and sizes. It entails facing fears of danger or risk to one's well-being or reputation to help others or a righteous cause. Courage can be physical, emotional, or intellectual, depending on the situation.

That lesson strengthened my Spiritual and Emotional pillars — reminding me that real courage often shows up in community, not in isolation.

#5. Life can be a win-win scenario

After my parents passed away, I was gratified to hear stories people would tell me about them. One theme that came through loud and clear about my Dad was that he believed in the win-win scenario and pursued it in all aspects of life. At work, he had a reputation for being a true diplomat (like that ambassador thing). I'm not sure if it was a natural gift or simply a lot of hard work and research, but he routinely brought people of opposing views together to find win-win outcomes. Too often in our culture, people think scenarios must boil down to winners and losers. Whether professional or personal, my Dad always aimed for a win-win scenario.

The final story I'd like to share is how he did this and how it played out wonderfully at his own funeral.

Nowhere is there more division than in the modern church. Like all mainline protestant denominations, the Episcopal Church is in decline. One of my father's last church-related responsibilities was co-chairing the search committee for a new Episcopal Bishop for the Diocese of Upper South Carolina. Let's set aside what defines the liberal-conservative division in the church. Suffice it to say my father (and his church) represented the conservative side in a broadly liberal denomination.

It quickly became apparent to my father early in the process that he would not be able to get his first-choice (or even second choice) candidate approved. Did he engage in a losing battle? No. He first sought a win-win by partnering with his co-chairman to agree that the long-term health of the church was a shared objective. Then, he focused his energy on securing the best possible candidate he could, someone who shared this objective and was, hopefully, willing to be the Bishop of the Diocese, not a narrative. But he didn't stop there.

He took the time to educate the candidate on the situation and what this candidate would face in a fractured church. They discussed common solutions that could lead to a successful tenure for the candidate. More importantly, after Bishop Waldo was confirmed, my Dad maintained an active mentoring relationship with him so that he might find success rather than resistance within the diocese. Win-win scenarios require both a successful strategy and follow-through.

When my parents passed away, I received an unexpected call from Bishop Waldo. He told me about the search and his experience with my Dad. Despite not being his first choice, he was forever grateful for my father's leadership, advocacy, and continued mentorship. He asked if he could participate in my parents' funeral. I could tell that the parish priest at my parents' church was concerned that the bishop might overstep. But all Bishop Waldo wanted to do was be there. He humbled himself by taking on a minor role to be present and to honor my mother and father, just as my father had humbled himself to successfully integrate Bishop Waldo into the church community.

My Dad taught me the heroic power of **Perseverance**: Heroes are determined and persistent in pursuing their goals. They do not give up easily, even in the face of setbacks or overwhelming odds.

That lesson strengthened my Intellectual, Emotional and Currencies pillars — showing me that perseverance paired with generosity creates lasting impact.

The world needs more heroes. In whatever form your post-sabbatical life takes shape, are you willing to aim a little higher to step up, lean in, and contribute your personal gifts and talents and be someone's hero?

Memento Mori is Latin for "remember you must die." What else do you want to accomplish, contribute to, and be remembered for before you do? What words do you want people to use when describing you? For the people he impacted and me, my Dad's heroic talents were captured in words like Integrity, Inspiration, Selflessness, Courage, and Perseverance.

We should all be so lucky.

Your Best Job Ever Awaits

Your best job ever — the one that began the day you picked up this book — is now yours to live. You have the tools, the stories, the systems, and the North Star. Go build the second act that only you can build. Build or repair what is broken with gold. Realign what is off course. And then step into the world as a hero it so badly needs.

The dividends will keep showing up for the rest of your life — and for everyone lucky enough to be touched by the life you choose to live.

Epilogue

Your Best Job Ever Is Just Getting Started

Take a minute and think back to the day you first picked up this book. Where were your head and heart? Uncertain? Burned out? Restless? Excited? Quietly anxious about what lay ahead?

I remember my own Day One clearly. Recall I was driving home from my in-laws, still exhausted, still carrying the weight of my old life, when that state trooper pulled me over for speeding. I was tight, uncertain, and running on fumes — but beneath it all I could already feel a new lightness. For the first time in years, I was ready to shed the old skin and begin something new.

Fast-forward to Day 321. The transformation was real. My SPiCE dashboard — which had flashed mostly red and yellow lights for so long — had turned green across the board. The hard work (and the fun) had paid off in ways I could see and feel every single day.

Here's one thing I've learned: It's relatively easy to think about taking a sabbatical. It's even easy to daydream about the things you might do. But thinking and dreaming are not enough. Real progress only happens when desire turns into deliberate, sustained action.

Your sabbatical will succeed or fail based on how fully you commit to doing the real work of realignment. That willingness to invest dedicated time and intentional effort in yourself is what turns this season into your best job ever.

With your strategy and plan now in hand, I envy the journey you're about to take. The waters ahead may be uncharted, but you're not sailing without a compass. You have your ERGO purpose to guide you, your SPiCE goals clearly charted, and your fulcrums ready to create powerful leverage.

Your best job ever is just getting started.

The Real Meaning of "Your Best Job Ever"

By now you understand one of the central ideas of this book: a sabbatical isn't a vacation — it's the most important job you'll ever have. The job of putting your life back in proper order.

The real meaning of "Your Best Job Ever" is not just what you do during the sabbatical, but who you become through the process. You will have fed and strengthened your five SPiCE pillars, creating a personal recipe that is authentically and powerfully you. You will have built resilience, clarity, and purpose that become jet fuel for the systems and habits that carry your goals and dreams forward.

At its heart, this work is about regaining full authority and autonomy over your life through what I call the Sovereignty Triangle:

Cognitive Sovereignty — the practice of independently evaluating the stories, assumptions, and information that come at you, rather than automatically accepting what the algorithm, media, or others feed you.

Body Sovereignty — taking ownership of your physical health, energy, strength, and well-being instead of outsourcing it to stress, over-promising quick fixes, poor habits, or the demands of daily life.

Spirit Sovereignty — reclaiming ownership of your inner life: your sense of meaning, purpose, values, and connection to something larger than yourself.

With these three forms of sovereignty operating in your back pocket, you step into the second half of your life with a level of resilience, clarity, and direction most people never fully develop.

That is the true gift of taking on your best job ever.

The Power of Ongoing Practice

Here's the truth most people miss: auditing your SPiCE is not a one-time exercise. It is an ongoing operating system.

The most successful Sabbaticaleers don't treat their SPiCE assessment like a box they check once and forget. They keep it alive as a regular dashboard, quietly checking in, spotting drift early, and making small course corrections before problems become crises. The real second act isn't built in one dramatic leap. It is built one intentional season at a time.

I learned this the same way I learned the power of systems from Scott Adams. Goals create what he calls "pre-success failure." Every day you haven't hit the target yet, you feel like you're failing, and that slow drip of discouragement wears you down. Systems are different. They turn good intentions into automatic behavior that compounds quietly over time. They shift your identity from "I'm trying to become the kind of person who..." to "This is simply what I do."

That's exactly how my own SPiCE practice evolved. During my sabbatical I tracked everything formally. Today it's far less rigid — more like my yoga practice or intermittent fasting. At first I measured and logged every session. Now those practices simply run in the background as part of who I am. The same thing happened with SPiCE and SWOT. They no longer feel like extra work. They've become quiet background software that helps me stay ahead of weakness and neutralize threats before they can derail me.

The real gift of your sabbatical is not just the time off. It's the repeatable system you now own — one that keeps you aligned, resilient, and moving forward for the rest of your life.

A Vision of What's Possible

Twelve to twenty four months from now, you'll look back and barely recognize the person who first picked up this book. You'll move through your days with a quiet confidence you haven't felt in years — clearer priorities, sharper perspective, and a steady inner alignment that no longer depends on external conditions. With renewed sovereignty across your mind, body, and spirit, you'll see every situation with fresh eyes and a deeper sense of power. As David R. Hawkins taught in Power vs. Force, true power flows from alignment, not force. When your image and identity are finally in harmony with who you really are, you stop pushing and start moving with the current.

Imagine returning to your previous job (or stepping into whatever comes next) not just "refreshed" like a vacation, but genuinely renewed. You show up with a complete sense of self — calm, focused, and operating from strength rather than depletion. Your presence alone becomes a quiet advantage, for you and for everyone around you. And when you look at your living dashboard, the transformation is unmistakable. Your Spiritual pillar carries a quiet, steady sense of alignment — decisions flow from a deeper "why" and life feels meaningful, not just busy. Your Physical pillar feels alive and capable again — energy rooted in sound sleep, movement that feels good, and sunlight on your skin. Your Intellectual pillar is reignited — curiosity returns as play, ideas spark easily, and your mind feels expansive. Your Currencies feel rich on your own terms — time with loved ones is abundant, experiences stack up that money can't buy, and relationships are deeper and more nourishing. And your Emotional pillar moves with grace — you feel joy, grief, anger, and tenderness fully, yet process them with resilience and peace, like clean air after a long rain.

These aren't distant ideals. They're the real, measurable payoff waiting for you when you read your SPiCE filter honestly and start acting on what it reveals.

Final Send-Off

As you embark on this exciting first chapter of your second act, remember this important truth: a sabbatical will change you, but it cannot change the world — only how you choose to interface with it.

In John 16:33, Jesus tells his disciples, "In this world you will have trouble..." We all face trials, regardless of our circumstances. What your renewed SPiCE dashboard, restored sovereignty, and intentional realignment give you is better armor and clearer direction as you move forward with purpose.

By all accounts, my maternal grandfather died a bitter and frustrated man. I'm not qualified to judge all the reasons why. I only saw the pain and dysfunction he left behind. Yet, I also know he believed deeply in the power of blessings.

I was his first grandchild. Shortly after I was born, he placed something special in a small drawer of an antique secretary — a pouch of pure-silver U.S. coins he had deliberately collected, knowing they would soon be taken out of circulation. Tucked inside was a handwritten note addressed to me. The drawer became stuck for decades. After he passed, when my mother and her siblings were dividing up his few belongings, they finally pried it open. Inside was that forgotten treasure — and his blessing to me:

To William Boy – Fair of hair with untold promise — I wish thee inner peace. Papa

That blessing has stayed with me my entire life, even before I knew it existed. I have never taken it for granted.

So dear reader, once and future Sabbaticaleer, I offer you my own blessing as you begin this journey:

May you have a grateful heart that stays open,
an equanimous mind that stays steady,
and a resilient body that feels strong, balanced, and truly at home in its own skin.

You've got everything you need.
Now go enjoy the best job you'll ever have.

And remember the rest of that verse from John 16:33 when Jesus continues with his own blessing: "But take heart! I have overcome the world."

Appendix I - Glossary

AM Reframe – A simple daily practice of being very intentional about the very first thing you consume each morning — whether meditation, prayer, or something else that sets a calm, centered frame. Because what you consume first thing will consume the rest of your day if you're not careful.

Autopilot – The set of automatic, unexamined patterns and reactions that shape how we live, often without our realizing it. Autopilot begins as perception—the fast, default story that feels true—and can quietly keep us stuck in old ways of thinking, relating, spending, moving, and meaning-making. The Autopilot Audit helps make these patterns visible so we can choose a more deliberate perspective.

Best Job Ever – My definition of a sabbatical: the best job you'll ever have, because the only employee is you and the work is rebuilding and realigning your own life for a successful second act.

Best Practices – Ten mindset resets for sabbatical success, starting with "Be Authentic" — practical rules to avoid common pitfalls and maximize your return on this once-in-a-lifetime investment.

Body Sovereignty – The personal right and practice of honoring and caring for your body as the sacred vessel that carries your entire life, instead of outsourcing it to chronic stress, default habits, quick pharmaceutical fixes, or unrealistic external standards. It's the foundation of sustained energy, vitality, and physical resilience during and after a sabbatical. It forms one of the three equal legs of *Sabbaticaleer's* Sovereignty Triangle. The Benefit: Builds sustained physical energy, vitality, strength, and resilience. Your body stops feeling like a problem to be fixed and becomes a trusted partner that supports the life you want to live.

Cognitive Sovereignty – The personal right and practice of independently evaluating the stories, assumptions, and information that come at you instead of automatically accepting what the algorithm, media, or others feed you. It's the foundation of clear thinking during and after a sabbatical. It forms one of the three equal legs of *Sabbaticaleer's* Sovereignty Triangle. The Benefit: Gives you clear, independent thinking and mental freedom. You stop living in someone else's narrative and begin writing your own.

ERGO – The four Strategic Sandboxes for sabbatical purpose: Exploration (wide-open discovery), Restoration (healing and recharge), Growth (deliberate expansion), and Objective (targeted achievement). You can choose one or blend two or three.

ERGO Anchors – The distilled, personal high-level purposes you choose from the ERGO sandboxes. They become the strategic direction for your entire sabbatical plan.

Eudaimonia – Aristotle's philosophy of lifelong intellectual and moral improvement through virtue, reason, meaningful activity, and relationships — a blueprint for a SPiCE-balanced, flourishing life.

Fulcrum – A high-impact activity or idea that intersects with multiple SPiCE pillars at once. These are the smart, leveraged moves that create the biggest positive shifts with the least wasted effort.

Ikigai – The Japanese concept of "reason for being" — the sweet spot where what you love, what you're good at, what the world needs, and what you can be rewarded for all overlap. It helps you find flow and meaning during and after your sabbatical.

Jubilee – The Biblical 50-year reset of debts and freedom, paralleling the mid-life reflection and fresh start that a sabbatical can provide.

Kintsugi (or Kintsukuroi) – The Japanese art of repairing broken pottery with gold lacquer. It celebrates the cracks and scars rather than hiding them — a powerful metaphor for sabbatical renewal through embracing our "scars of life."

Living Dashboard – Your ongoing system of journal entries, SWOT analysis, and regular SPiCE snapshots that keeps you honest and lets you see real shifts in real time.

Metanoia – Drawn from Mark's Gospel, this is a profound change of heart and mind — not just feeling sorry, but releasing old patterns and walking in a new direction. It's the emotional turning point that creates lasting renewal.

Metrics Dashboard – Ongoing sabbatical tracking: journal, SWOT, and SPiCE snapshots — for accountability and course corrections.

Neuroplasticity – The brain's ability to rewire itself through new experiences, enabling the intellectual growth and adaptability that a sabbatical can unlock.

North Star Statement – A short, memorable sentence or two that captures the guiding idea or legacy you want to live by. It becomes your personal compass once the sabbatical ends.

Power-Based Rebranding – The intentional process of shedding an old image and stepping into a truer identity that reflects who you've become after your sabbatical. It's about aligning how the world sees you with who you actually are.

Pre-Sabbatical Baseline – Your SPiCE score before your sabbatical. It serves as the starting-line metric to help prioritize your planning and track your progress.

Quiet Thieves – The small, everyday habits and thought patterns — like endless scrolling, people-pleasing, comparison, overthinking, and living on autopilot — that quietly steal your Cognitive, Body, and Spirit sovereignty without you even noticing.

Sabbatical – 1) A defined period, intentionally focused on comprehensive recovery and renewal, resulting in a purposeful, personal realignment for successful second acts of life. 2) Your Best Job Ever.

Sabbatical Cues – Quiet or loud signals (burnout, loss, itch for more) that prompt a pause to realign.

Sabbaticaleer – A person who intentionally designs and executes a successful sabbatical to renew their SPiCE pillars, realign with purpose, and step powerfully into life's second act.

Second Act – The renewed, purposeful and long lasting life phase that follows your sabbatical, built on realignment and resilience.

Shemitah – The Biblical seventh-year land rest for renewal, mirroring the trust in abundance and the power of pause that a sabbatical provides.

SPiCE – The five core pillars of personal well-being: Spiritual, Physical, Intellectual, Currencies, and Emotional — the foundation for assessing and shifting your life during sabbatical and beyond.

SPiCE Goals – Measurable goals established for each SPiCE pillar to drive meaningful change. These goals are based on what you need most from your sabbatical — with at least one primary goal per pillar (and optional secondary goals for added depth). Their purpose is to create clear, positive shifts that support your realignment and long-term renewal.

Spiritual SPiCE – The inner spark of purpose and meaning: reconnecting with values, faith, awe, or self-reflection to stay pointed true north.

Physical SPiCE – Your vibrant vessel for life: honoring the body through strength, energy, resilience, and habits that ditch the grind before it drains you dry.

Intellectual SPiCE – Your curious mind in action: feeding hunger for new ideas, challenging old views, and igniting lifelong learning to keep the brain sharp and adaptable.

Currencies SPiCE – What you treasure: beyond finances, including relationships, experiences, time, and qualities that leave you feeling genuinely fulfilled.

Emotional SPiCE – Your inner steadiness for the storms: navigating feelings with grace, building peace, and bouncing back stronger without breaking.

Strategic Filter – Running your sabbatical cues and ideas through SPiCE and ERGO to craft a purposeful, balanced plan.

Strategy Brief – A 1–2 page living document that assembles your sabbatical: purpose, SPiCE goals, fulcrums, itinerary, timing, logistics, and legacy.

Sovereignty Triangle – Sabbaticaleer's simple but powerful framework consisting of three equal legs — Cognitive Sovereignty, Body Sovereignty, and Spirit Sovereignty. It is the deeper idea behind SPiCE — the deliberate act of taking back full ownership of your mind, body, and spirit, rather than outsourcing them to stress, distraction, or default habits.

Spirit Sovereignty – The personal right and practice of staying deeply connected to your own sense of purpose, values, awe, and something greater than yourself, instead of outsourcing meaning to external approval, cultural noise, or constant busyness. It's the foundation of inner peace and a centered, purposeful life during and after a sabbatical. It forms one of the three equal legs of *Sabbaticaleer's* Sovereignty Triangle. The Benefit: Creates a steady sense of inner peace and a centered, purposeful life. You stop looking outside yourself for validation and begin living from a quiet, unshakable inner compass.

SWOT Analysis – A strategic snapshot: Strengths (leverage), Weaknesses (shore up), Opportunities (chase), Threats (watch) for sabbatical planning.

Tent Pole Adventures – Big, memorable experiences that anchor your sabbatical itinerary, like a multi-week trip or major project.

Wabi-Sabi – The Japanese philosophy of finding beauty in imperfection, impermanence, and the natural cycle of growth, decay, and renewal. It becomes a guiding lens for embracing your own "survivor patina" and authentic second-act renewal.

Appendix II – The Sovereignty Triangle & Journal Prompts

The Sovereignty Triangle

The Sovereignty Triangle is the bigger idea behind SPiCE. While SPiCE gives you an honest dashboard of where you stand, the Sovereignty Triangle turns those five pillars into a complete system of reclaimed and realigned personal ownership. It is built on three equal legs:

Together, the Sovereignty Triangle is the deliberate act of taking back full ownership of your mind (choosing where you invest your mental energy instead of letting a career, algorithms or others run the show), your body (stepping off the hamster wheel of quick fixes, pills, and the pressure to outsource your health to anything outside yourself), and your spirit (finding the confidence to embrace your true purpose and faith even in a judgmental world) instead of quietly outsourcing them to stress, distraction, or default habits.

The real benefit is lasting clarity of mind, sustained physical energy and resilience, and a steady inner peace that extends far beyond your sabbatical.

Below you'll find a clear definition, the key benefits, the most common "Quiet Thieves" that steal each form of sovereignty, and a practical set of journal exercises for each leg. Use them as an à la carte menu — pick what feels alive right now, and return to them often.

Cognitive Sovereignty

Definition – The personal right and practice of independently evaluating the stories, assumptions, and information that come at you instead of automatically accepting what the algorithm, media, or others feed you.

Benefits – Gives you clear, independent thinking and mental freedom. You stop living in someone else's narrative and begin writing your own.

Quiet Thieves

- The endless (and often mendacious) algorithm feed designed to keep you engaged, outraged, or reassured
- Cultural and social pressure to adopt popular opinions without examination
- Old mental habits and confirmation bias that feel comfortable but keep you small
- Echo chambers and tribal thinking that reinforce

existing beliefs while shielding us from any perspective that might challenge them

Journal Exercises – Cognitive Sovereignty Menu

(These are the same prompts that appear at the end of Chapter 2 for easy reference.)

These prompts help you examine the stories, assumptions, and information you've been living inside. Pick one or two that feel alive right now, grab your journal, and explore on your own terms.

Quiet Thief 1 – The endless (and often mendacious) algorithm feed

1. **The Algorithm Audit** – Look at your main social media or news feeds. What emotions do they most often provoke – outrage, fear, reassurance, or comparison? How does that emotional pull shape what you believe?

2. **The Engagement Trap** – When was the last time you kept scrolling because something made you angry or anxious? What would it look like to step away from the algorithm and think for yourself?

3. **Curating Your Input** – If you could design your own information diet free from algorithmic manipulation, what sources or practices would you choose instead?

4. **The Outrage Test** – Pick one story that recently triggered a strong emotional reaction in your feed. Ask

yourself: "Is this information complete, or am I being emotionally steered?" Write what you discover.

Quiet Thief 2 – Cultural and social pressure to adopt popular opinions without examination

1. **The Popular Opinion Check** – What belief or viewpoint do you hold mainly because it's widely accepted in your social circle? How would you feel if you questioned it?

2. **The Fear of Disagreeing** – Where do you stay silent or go along with the group even when something doesn't feel right to you? What small step could you take toward intellectual honesty?

3. The Soc**ial Pressure Mirror** – Think of a recent conversation where you felt pressure to agree. What would it have looked like to speak your own truth instead?

4. **Independent Thinking Practice** – Choose one current cultural or political topic. Research it and write down your honest view — not what you think you "should" believe, but what you actually think after careful consideration.

Quiet Thief 3 – Old mental habits and confirmation bias that feel comfortable but keep you small

1. **The Confirmation Bias Check** – When was the last time you only sought out information that confirmed what you already believed? How did that limit your thinking?

2. **The Comfortable Story** – What old mental habit or assumption about yourself or the world feels safe but may be holding you back? Write it down, then write the opposite view.

3. **Intellectual Humility** – Think of a belief you've held for years. What evidence would it take for you to reconsider it? Are you truly open to that evidence?

4. **The Growth Question** – What is one assumption you've been carrying that might no longer serve you? What would change if you released it and thought freshly about the topic?

Quiet Thief 4 – Echo chambers and tribal thinking

1. **The Tribal Mirror** – Where do you notice yourself automatically aligning with your group's view without independently examining the evidence? What might open up if you stepped outside that circle for a moment?

2. **Seeking the Other Side** – Pick a topic you feel strongly about. Deliberately seek out a thoughtful, well-reasoned argument from the opposing perspective. What shifts (if any) occur in your thinking?

3. **Breaking the Bubble** – What sources, people, or communities do you tend to avoid because they challenge your current beliefs? What could happen if you engaged with them honestly?

4. **Loyalty vs Truth** – Is there an area in your life

where group loyalty feels more important to you than pursuing truth? What would intellectual honesty look like in that area?

Body Sovereignty

Definition – The personal right and practice of honoring and caring for your body as the sacred vessel that carries your entire life instead of outsourcing it to chronic stress, default habits, quick pharmaceutical fixes, or unrealistic external standards.

Benefits – Builds sustained physical energy, vitality, strength, and resilience. Your body stops feeling like a problem to be fixed and becomes a trusted partner that supports the life you want to live.

Quiet Thieves

- Cultural norms and the beauty/performance industrial complex that tell you your body is never quite good enough

- The "pill for everything" mindset that outsources discomfort instead of listening to what your body is asking for

- Hustle culture that glorifies pushing through exhaustion and ignoring signals of pain or fatigue

- Self-abdication — the quiet choice to numb, distract, or override your body's needs with habits that feel easier in the moment

Journal Exercises – Body Sovereignty Menu

These prompts shift your relationship with your physical self from criticism or outsourcing to honest ownership and care. They focus on tracking energy and sleep, listening to tension and signals, making conscious choices around nourishment and boundaries, practicing stillness and self-appreciation, and envisioning the strong, resilient body you want to carry into the second half of life.

Quiet Thief 1. Cultural Norms & the Beauty/Performance Industrial Complex –These prompts help you examine how external standards have shaped your perceptions and treatment of your body.

1. **The Comparison Trap** – Where do you catch yourself measuring your body against media, social media, or fitness culture? How does that comparison make you feel, and what would it look like to stop playing that game?

2. **The "Never Enough" Story** – What specific messages have you internalized about your body not being good enough? Write them down, then write a compassionate counter-statement you can return to.

3. **The Beauty Standard Audit** – List three ways you've tried to "fix" or improve your body to meet external ideals. Which efforts actually served you, and which quietly stole your peace?

4. **Body as Worth** – If your body didn't have to look a certain way to be "acceptable," how would you treat it

differently today?

Quiet Thief 2. The "Pill for Everything" Mindset – These prompts encourage you to listen to your body's signals instead of automatically outsourcing discomfort.

1. **The Signal vs. Symptom Check** – Think of a recent physical discomfort (pain, fatigue, tension). Did you reach for a quick fix first, or did you pause to ask what your body was trying to tell you?

2. **The Quick Fix Inventory** – What discomforts do you regularly numb or medicate rather than address at the root? What might change if you chose curiosity over relief?

3. **Listening First** – Before reaching for any pill, supplement, or distraction the next time you feel off, sit with the feeling for five minutes. What does your body actually need?

4. **Reclaiming Responsibility** – Write a short commitment: "I choose to listen to my body before I outsource its care." What small step could you take this week to live that out?

Quiet Thief 3. Hustle Culture – These prompts challenge the glorification of pushing through exhaustion.

1. **The Push-Through Pattern** – When was the last time you ignored fatigue, pain, or burnout and kept going anyway? What did that cost you?

2. **The Rest Question** – Where in your life are you still

equating rest with laziness? What would it look like to treat rest as a responsible, powerful choice?

3. **The Exhaustion Warning Signs** – List the early signals your body gives when it's overwhelmed. How can you honor those signals instead of overriding them?

4. **Sustainable Energy** – What would a day or week look like if you respected your body's need for recovery as much as its need for output?

Quiet Thief 4. Self-Abdication – These prompts address the quiet ways we numb, distract, or override our body's needs.

1. **The Numbing Habit** – What habits do you turn to when your body is asking for attention (scrolling, snacking, overworking, etc.)? What are you really trying to avoid feeling?

2. **The Override** – When was the last time you told your body "not now" when it clearly needed something? What would it have looked like to listen instead?

3. **The Easy Choice Audit** – Look at your daily routines. Where are you choosing what feels easier in the moment over what your body actually needs for the long term?

4. **Reclaiming Agency** – Write a short promise to yourself: "From now on, when my body speaks, I will..." Finish the sentence and commit to one small action this week.

Spirit Sovereignty

Definition – The personal right and practice of staying deeply connected to your own sense of purpose, values, awe, and something greater than yourself instead of outsourcing meaning to external approval, cultural noise, or constant busyness.

Benefits – Creates a steady sense of inner peace and a centered, purposeful life. You stop looking outside yourself for validation and begin living from a quiet, unshakable inner compass.

Quiet Thieves

- The constant need for external approval and the fear of being judged
- Cultural noise and the pressure to adopt other people's definitions of success and meaning
- Busyness and distraction that keep you from sitting with the deeper questions
- Old stories of unworthiness or "not enough" that quietly erode your sense of purpose

Journal Exercises – Spirit Sovereignty Menu

These prompts help you reconnect with purpose, values, and something greater than yourself. They explore what makes you feel most alive, clarify your core values, cultivate awe and gratitude, release judgment and external expectations, trust your inner compass, and reflect on the legacy you hope to leave.

Quiet Thief 1. The constant need for external approval and the fear of being judged

1. **The Approval Trap** – Where are you still making decisions based on what others might think? What would change if you released the fear of judgment and trusted your own inner compass?

2. **Validation Check** – When was the last time you sought external approval before trusting your own knowing? How did that feel, and what would it look like to choose inner validation instead?

3. **The Fear of Judgment** – What part of your true self are you still hiding because you fear being judged? What would it look like to let that part see the light?

4. **Inner vs Outer Approval** – Write a letter to yourself giving the approval and acceptance you've been seeking from others. What does your inner voice want to say?

Quiet Thief 2. Cultural noise and the pressure to adopt other people's definitions of success and meaning

1. **The Success Comparison** – Where have you adopted someone else's definition of success or a meaningful life as your own? How does that definition feel when you sit with it quietly?

2. **The Noise Audit** – What cultural messages about success and meaning are loudest in your life right now? Which of those messages feel true to you, and which

do not?

3. **Reclaiming Your Definition** – If no one else's opinion mattered, how would you define a meaningful and successful life for yourself?

4. **The External Compass** – Where are you still letting society, family, or culture dictate what your life "should" look like? What would it feel like to hand the compass back to your own spirit?

Quiet Thief 3. Busyness and distraction that keep you from sitting with the deeper questions

1. **The Busyness Barrier** – How does constant busyness keep you from sitting with the deeper questions of purpose and meaning? What would one small pocket of stillness look like this week?

2. **The Distraction Inventory** – What habits or distractions do you turn to when the deeper questions feel uncomfortable? What might you discover if you sat with those questions instead?

3. **Creating Sacred Space** – What would it look like to protect one small window of time each week for quiet reflection and connection to something greater?

4. **The Deeper Question** – What is one big question about your purpose or life direction that you've been avoiding? Write it down and sit with it for ten minutes without trying to answer it.

Quiet Thief 4. Old stories of unworthiness or "not enough" that quietly erode your sense of purpose

1. **The Not Enough Story** – What old story of unworthiness or "not enough" still whispers to you? How has that story limited your sense of purpose?

2. **The Worthiness Audit** – Where do you still feel you have to earn your right to exist or to pursue what matters to you? What would it feel like to release that burden?

3. **Rewriting the Old Story** – Write the old unworthiness story you've carried, then write a new, compassionate story that honors your inherent worth and purpose.

4. **The Inner Knowing** – When have you felt a quiet sense of "I am enough" or "I belong here"? What conditions allowed that feeling to arise, and how can you create them more often?

How to Use These Exercises

Treat them as an à la carte menu. Pick one or two that feel alive right now. Return to them often — especially once you're on sabbatical and have the dedicated time and space to go deeper. The goal is not perfection. The goal is ownership.

The Sovereignty Triangle is not something you master in a weekend. It is a lifelong practice of choosing, again and again, to live as the author of your own life rather than a character in someone else's story.

You now have the map. The real journey — and the real freedom — begins when you start walking it.

Appendix III - Selected Sabbatical Reading

Looking for sabbatical reading material? Here are selections from my sabbatical.

Spiritual – *Focus on Growth*

Serving with Eyes Wide Open – Doing Short-Term Missions with Cultural Intelligence by David A.Livermore

This book was recommended to us before my men's group's mission trip to Ecuador. Livermore offers a refreshingly honest and practical look at the real scope, nature, and limitations of short-term mission trips. Instead of the typical "go save the world" enthusiasm, he challenges readers to approach service with cultural intelligence, humility, realistic expectations, and genuine respect for the people and communities being served.

For anyone considering a mission trip or any form of service during their sabbatical, this is essential reading. It will help you serve more effectively and respectfully while protecting both your own heart and the dignity of those you hope to help.

Man's Search For Meaning by Victor Frankl

Viktor Frankl's *Man's Search for Meaning* is a profound memoir and psychological work based on his experiences as a prisoner in Nazi concentration camps during World War II. In the midst of unimaginable suffering, Frankl discovered that the primary human drive is not pleasure or power, but the search for meaning. He developed logotherapy, showing that we can find meaning through our work, our love for others, or the courageous attitude we take toward unavoidable suffering — and that this search for meaning is what ultimately sustains us.

Mere Christianity by C.S. Lewis

Originally written as a series of radio broadcasts the British government asked Lewis to deliver during the darkest days of the London Blitz, *Mere Christianity* is one of the most accessible and powerful explanations of the Christian faith ever written. With quiet logic, dry humor, and deep insight, Lewis lays out the case for what he calls "mere" Christianity — the core beliefs that have united Christians across denominations for centuries.

For anyone on sabbatical seeking spiritual clarity and a stronger inner compass, this book is pure gold. It's the perfect blend of intellectual rigor and heartfelt wisdom — and yes, C.S. Lewis was basically the original podcaster, delivering life-changing ideas straight into people's living rooms while bombs fell overhead.

The Bible

Setting aside that *The Bible* is God's divine revelation to Humanity, at its core, *The Bible* is the ultimate field guide for renewal, realignment, and stepping into a new chapter of life — exactly what a sabbatical is all about. From the ancient rhythm of Sabbath rest and the seventh-year *Shemitah* pause to the sweeping reset of *Jubilee*, Scripture repeatedly shows us that dedicated seasons of stopping, reflecting, and trusting are not luxuries — they are essential for a life of purpose and strength.

Whether you're seeking wisdom, comfort, direction, or simply a deeper sense of your inner compass, *The Bibl*e offers timeless truths for each SPiCE pillar. If you've never read *The Bible*, a sabbatical is a wonderful excuse and opportunity to finally do so. It's not just a religious text; it's a practical companion for anyone doing the best job they'll ever have — redesigning their life for a purposeful and lasting second act.

Physical – *Focus on Health & Wellness*

Power vs Force – The Hidden Determinants of Human Behavior by David R. Hawkins, M.D., P h.D.

This is a tough yet deeply satisfying read that will challenge how you see yourself, your decisions, and the world around you. Using muscle testing and a calibrated scale of human consciousness, Hawkins reveals the invisible forces that drive human behavior — distinguishing "Power" (aligned, life-giving energy) from "Force" (ego-driven, ultimately depleting energy).

In the context of a sabbatical, this book becomes a powerful mirror. It helps you examine where you've been operating from force versus true power and gives you a practical framework for raising your own level of consciousness. It ties directly into Cognitive Sovereignty and the Sovereignty Triangle, showing how realignment at the deepest level creates lasting change across every SPiCE pillar.

If you're willing to do the work, Power vs. Force can become one of the most transformative books you read during your sabbatical.

Intellectual – *Focus on Wisdom*

How to Fail at Almost Everything and Still Win Big: Kind of the Story of My Life by Scott Adams

Scott Adams, the creator of Dilbert, delivers one of the most practical and entertaining books on success ever written. His central message is simple but profound: forget about setting big goals. Goals create what he calls "pre-success failure" — that constant feeling of falling short that slowly wears you down. Instead, build systems — repeatable processes that compound quietly over time and shift your identity from "I'm trying to become..." to "This is simply what I do."

In the context of *Sabbaticaleer*, this book is pure gold. It perfectly reinforces why SPiCE is designed as a lifelong operating system rather than a one-time checklist. Your sabbatical is the perfect time to stop chasing distant goals and start installing the daily systems that will carry you through a purposeful and lasting second act.

If you want a funny, no-nonsense push to stop relying on willpower and start building the habits and frameworks that actually work, this is the book for you.

The Intelligent Investor – the Definitive Book on Value Investing by Benjamin Graham

This is the classic book on value investing, written by Benjamin Graham (the man Warren Buffett calls his teacher and the "father of value investing"). It teaches timeless principles of patience, discipline, emotional control, and independent thinking — focusing on long-term value rather than short-term market noise.

In the context of *Sabbaticaleer*, *The Intelligent Investor* is much more than a book about money. It's a masterclass in clear thinking, strategic patience, and making wise, high-ROI decisions — skills that directly strengthen your Intellectual and Currencies SPiCE pillars. It was recommended to me by several people, most notably my financial advisors, Lige and Mark, and it became one of the most valuable books I read during my sabbatical.

If you want to sharpen your mind, improve your decision-making, and learn how to think long-term in every area of life, this book is essential reading.

Dune by Frank Herbert

Frank Herbert's epic masterpiece *Dune* is widely regarded as one of the greatest science fiction novels ever written. Set on the harsh desert planet Arrakis, it follows young Paul Atreides as he navigates treacherous politics, ecological realities, spiritual awakening, and his own emerging destiny.

During a sabbatical, *Dune* becomes a powerful intellectual journey. It challenges you to think strategically over long time horizons, cultivate mental discipline in the face of extreme uncertainty, and see the complex, interconnected systems that shape reality. As you follow Paul Atreides' profound transformation from an uncertain young man into a figure of great consequence, the story quietly mirrors the inner work many experience during a well-designed sabbatical — questioning old identities and stepping into a larger sense of purpose.

If you're ready to stretch your mind and explore big ideas about leadership, resilience, and becoming who you are truly meant to be, *Dune* is a deeply rewarding intellectual companion for your sabbatical. It's one of my favorites and inspired my own use of the word and framework of SPiCE.

The Book of Proverbs

One of the most practical and timeless books in the Bible, *Proverbs* is a collection of wise sayings on how to live skillfully, make sound decisions, and build a life of integrity and long-term success. Attributed largely to King Solomon, it offers straightforward guidance on everything from discipline and self-control to the dangers of pride, laziness, and bad company.

In the context of *Sabbaticaleer*, Proverbs is an outstanding intellectual companion for your sabbatical. It sharpens your thinking, strengthens your judgment, and encourages the kind of deep, adaptable wisdom that supports a strong Intellectual SPiCE pillar. Many of its teachings help you develop the long-term thinking and prudent decision-making needed to design a purposeful second act.

If you want ancient, battle-tested wisdom to guide your realignment and future direction, Proverbs is one of the best places you can turn.

Currencies – Focus on Priorities

Your Money or Your Life by Vicki Robin and Joe Domingo

This groundbreaking book was given to me by my father as I entered the workforce, and it completely changed how I think about money, time, and life energy. It teaches you to treat every dollar as a unit of your life energy, calculate your true hourly wage, and consciously decide what "enough" really means so you can stop trading your life for things you don't actually need.

In the context of *Sabbaticaleer*, Your Money or Your Life is essential reading for the Currencies pillar. It helps you examine your relationship with money with radical honesty and clarity, empowering you to design a sabbatical (and a second act) that aligns with your deepest values rather than societal expectations.

It's a powerful tool for reclaiming your time, freedom, and life energy so that your sabbatical becomes a true investment in a purposeful and lasting second act.

Raising a Modern-Day Knight: A Father's Role in Guiding His Son to Authentic Manhood by Robert Lewis

We studied this at my Ironmen Men's Group, where I've led a table for over 15 years now. It offers a powerful, practical framework for parents who want to intentionally raise their children with character, purpose, and a clear vision of what it means to be a people of integrity.

In the context of *Sabbaticaleer*, this book is a meaningful addition to the Currencies pillar. It reminds us that one of the greatest treasures we can invest in is the next generation — our legacy through our children. A sabbatical provides the time and space to reflect deeply on how we show up as parents, what values we want to pass on, and how we can be more present and purposeful in our most important relationships.

If you're a parent (or hope to be), this book will challenge and equip you to approach parenthood with greater clarity and intentionality — a key part of building a rich, fulfilling second act

Atomic Habits by James Clear

James Clear's *Atomic Habits* is one of the most practical and influential books on behavior change ever written. Clear shows how tiny, consistent improvements — atomic habits — compound into remarkable results over time. He makes a powerful distinction between goals and systems, teaching that you don't rise to the level of your goals — you fall to the level of your systems. By focusing on small daily habits and shifting your identity, you turn good intentions into automatic behaviors that stick.

In the context of *Sabbaticaleer*, this book is a game-changer for the Currencies pillar. Your sabbatical gives you the rare time and mental space to intentionally redesign your daily routines around what truly matters — your time, energy, relationships, and personal fulfillment. Whether it's protecting your mornings, moving your body consistently, deepening connections with loved ones, or simply showing up more present, Atomic Habits gives you the practical framework to build the repeatable systems that support a rich, purposeful second act long after your sabbatical ends.

Emotional – Focus in Resilience and Alignment

A Resilient Life – You Can Move Ahead No Matter What by Gordon MacDonald

Gordon MacDonald's *A Resilient Life* is a deeply practical and encouraging guide to building emotional and spiritual endurance that lasts. Drawing on Scripture, personal stories, and hard-won wisdom, MacDonald shows how to develop the inner strength needed to keep moving forward when life gets hard — not by denying pain, but by learning how to process it with honesty and grace.

In the context of *Sabbaticaleer*, this book is a powerful companion for the Emotional pillar. My friend, Pastor Chuck, and I read it together and discussed it chapter by chapter during a couple of very challenging months, well after my sabbatical ended. It helped me navigate the inevitable "In this world you will have trouble" turbulence and taught me how to build the kind of resilience that doesn't just help you survive hard seasons — it helps you grow stronger through them.

If you want to leave your sabbatical with the emotional tools to handle whatever comes next — whether it's joy, disappointment, transition, or the normal ups and downs of life — this book belongs on your list.

The Great Gatsby, by F. Scott Fitzgerald (1925)

A classic American novel and one of the most powerful stories ever written about the destructive gap between image and identity. On the surface, Jay Gatsby appears to have everything — wealth, status, and a carefully crafted persona — yet his relentless pursuit of an illusion leaves him empty and ultimately destroyed.

In the context of *Sabbaticaleer*, *The Great Gatsby* is a sobering and valuable read for the Currencies pillar. It forces you to examine the difference between how the world sees you and who you truly are. The book shows, with haunting clarity, what happens when we chase the wrong kind of "wealth" — when image is prioritized over authentic identity, when external success is pursued at the expense of real relationships and inner alignment. A sabbatical is the perfect time to step back and ask the hard question Gatsby never did: Am I building a life that is genuinely rich, or just one that looks rich?

Worth reading on its own as great literature, *The Great Gatsby* also serves as a cautionary tale that makes the work you're doing in this book even more meaningful.

Frankenstein, by Mary Shelley (1818)

Mary Shelley's *Frankenstein* is a timeless classic and one of the most haunting explorations of ambition, responsibility, and the emotional cost of creation ever written. At its heart, it tells the story of Victor Frankenstein, who brings a being to life but then abandons it, leaving his creation to wrestle with profound isolation, rejection, and an aching search for identity and purpose.

In the context of *Sabbaticaleer*, this novel is a powerful mirror for the Emotional pillar. It forces you to examine the gap between what you create (a career, an image, a life) and how you care for what you've created — including yourself. The monster's descent into rage and despair shows what happens when emotional needs are ignored and identity is left unformed. A sabbatical gives you the rare space to do the opposite: to face your own "creations," take responsibility for them, and begin the work of healing, integration, and authentic self-acceptance.

Worth reading on its own as great literature, *Frankenstein* also serves as a sobering reminder of why emotional realignment is one of the most important parts of building a purposeful second act.

Acknowledgements

I could not have written this book without the love and support of so many people.

First and foremost, my beautiful wife Elizabeth and our amazing children, William and Grace — thank you for walking this journey with me and for giving me the space and encouragement to pursue it.

To my brother Dave Thomason — my fellow traveler through loss and healing, and the one who turned me on to the subtle beauty of *survivor patina*. Our shared love of classic Mercedes has been one of the great joys of the second act.

To my mother and father-in-law, Sally and Bill Cowan, for their steady love and support through it all.

To my brother-in-law Bart Thrasher, who always lent an ear when times were tough.

To Pastor Chuck Roberts, who walked with me on Resilience Road

To my iron-brother Glenn Harvin, who kept asking the question that started it all: "What are you doing for you?"

To my weekly Ironmen table — for years of faith, accountability, and raw authenticity.

To Jane P.W. and Mila B. – twin pillars of my yoga tutelage along with my fellow yoga bros and the larger community at

LifeTime— thank you for the friendship, the insights, and the daily lessons in gratitude, equanimity, and resilience.

To Dr. Andy Ward, my sounding board for objectivity and accountability.

To Lige Gillis and Mark Rebillot, our trusted financial advisors, who give me the confidence and freedom to stay focused on the Currencies in my life that truly matter.

To Richard Ward, my last boss, who looked me in the eye and said, "Sabbatical will be the best job you'll ever have."

And finally, to my Lord and Savior Jesus Christ — the ultimate source of strength, hope, and renewal.

Thank you all.

About the author

Will Thomason spent nearly 30 years in advertising, helping companies and brands reimagine their identities and craft strategies that delivered real results. After burnout and the sudden loss of his parents, he took a 321-day intentional sabbatical to heal, realign, and redesign his life for the second half.

That journey became the foundation for *Sabbaticaleer*. Drawing on his strategy and branding expertise as well as personal experience, Will created the SPiCE framework, ERGO sandboxes, and the Sovereignty Triangle — practical tools that help readers get an honest read on where they stand, define a meaningful direction, and take back full ownership of their mind, body, and spirit.

Today, he continues to live the systems he writes about. He remains active in his church and men's group, maintains a long-running yoga practice, and regularly checks his SPiCE dashboard to stay aligned. He has restored a barn-find 1970 Mercedes-Benz 280SL Pagoda — a near-perfect metaphor for his own personal renewal — while bonding with his brother Dave over their shared love of classic Mercedes. He lives in Atlanta, Georgia, with his wife, Elizabeth. Together, they are straddling the empty nest with their two adult children, William and Grace.

He hopes readers finish the book feeling realigned, equipped with practical tools, and quietly confident that they too can design a sabbatical that becomes their best job ever — and create a purposeful, lasting second act.

www.ingramcontent.com/pod-product-compliance
Lightning Source LLC
LaVergne TN
LVHW010650110826
845149LV00014B/3012

* 9 7 9 8 9 9 6 0 2 7 9 1 0 *